**FATE Presents**

# CONTACT WITH THE DEAD

FATE Presents

# CONTACT WITH THE DEAD

Compiled & Edited by

Rosemary Ellen Guiley

Visionary Living Publishing/Visionary Living, Inc.
New Milford, Connecticut

*Fate Presents*
*Contact with the Dead*

Compiled and edited by Rosemary Ellen Guiley

Copyright Visionary Living, Inc. 2018

Front cover design by April Page Slaughter
Back cover and interior design by Leslie McAllister

ISBN: 978-1-942157-35-9 (pbk)
ISBN: 978-1-942157-36-6 (epub)

Visionary Living Publishing/Visionary Living, Inc.
New Milford, Connecticut
www.visionarylivingpublishing.com

# TABLE OF CONTENTS

# Introduction

Throughout history, the living have had contact with the dead, and have left testimonies behind them for subsequent generations to ponder and examine. Most experiences are spontaneous and may happen only once or twice. We have also developed the ability for regular contact through various forms of mediumship and technology.

Maintaining a connection to those who pass on is vitally important to humanity – consider all our customs and rituals, worldwide since antiquity, aimed at honoring the dead and reaching out to the Other Side. Our efforts help both the dead and ourselves, giving us reassurance that death doesn't bring an end to us but ushers in a new phase of existence.

Modern science may still waver on "proof" of contact, but for most people who have had an experience, the proof of survival after death and the continuing life of loved ones in another realm is powerful, personal and unshakeable.

FATE magazine has been publishing since 1948, covering all things mysterious and unexplained. Topics of great importance throughout the magazine's history include survival after death, the afterlife, and communication with the dead. Leading experts, researchers and mediums, as well as everyday people, have contributed articles and experiences that inform and reassure a worldwide audience.

This anthology, and its sister companion, *Fate Presents Mysteries of the Afterlife*, are collections of articles that address important aspects of what we know and experience about the Other Side.

There are 31 articles grouped in four sections:

**Dreams and Visitations** features two of the most common ways we have contact with the dead. One is through extraordinary dreams that enable the transmission of farewells, reassurances and last messages. The other is through waking visions and sensations.

**Mediumship** takes a look at how mediums receive information and impressions from the dead, from verbal messages to inspiration for writing and painting. Included are interesting cases, and tips for conducting seances and establishing links.

**Technology Communication** covers how technology has been employed to establish audio and visual communication, even in real-time. Tips for collecting your own evidence are provided. Some of the technology has changed; for example, magnetic tape recorders have given way to digital recorders, but the techniques are still similar or the same.

**Contact and Visitations from Pets** features articles on one of the most poignant aspects of survival, our profound love for our pets. They do make return visits from the afterlife, just like people.

I have included the date and issue of the articles. Most, but not all, also have short bios of the authors. I have included some of my own FATE articles as well and have augmented the FATE collection with a few of my pieces from outside FATE which address significant topics. The result is an absorbing collection of articles with historical and contemporary relevance.

Some of the articles feature drawings and photographs, which have been taken from the original copies of FATE. For most of its history, FATE has been printed on coarse newsprint paper, and so the quality of the images varies.

If you have ever had contact with the dead – or desire to do so – you will find these well-researched articles a welcome addition to your knowledge.

– Rosemary Ellen Guiley, Executive Editor, FATE

# DREAMS AND VISITATIONS

# AFTER-DEATH COMMUNICATION
## Bill and Judy Guggenheim

*[Bill and Judy Guggenheim created the ADC (After-Death Communication) Project in May 1988. They interviewed 2,000 people in 50 states and 10 Canadian provinces. Ranging in age from children to the elderly, the respondents represent diverse social, educational, economic, occupational and religious backgrounds. It is estimated that at least 50 million Americans, or 20 percent of the population, have had one or more experiences with after-death communication. The following is adapted from The ADC Project.]*

## The 12 most frequent types of after-death communication

### 1. Sensing a presence
You have a distinct feeling that your loved one is nearby, even though he or she can't be seen or heard. This is the most common form of contact, but many people discount these experiences, thinking, "Oh, I'm just

imagining this." Presences are most often felt during the days and weeks immediately after a death; however, a presence may be sensed months and even years later.

### 2. Hearing a voice
Some people say they hear an external voice, just as when a living person speaks to them. However, most communication is by telepathy – heard in the mind. It's possible to have an entire conversation this way.

### 3. Feeling a touch
You may feel your loved one touch you with his or her hand or place an arm around your shoulders or back for comfort and reassurance. You may feel a tap, a pat, a caress, a stroke, a kiss or even a hug.

### 4. Smelling a fragrance
You may smell your relative's or friend's favorite cologne, after-shave lotion or perfume. Other common scents include flowers (especially roses), bath powders, tobacco products, favorite foods and personal scents.

### 5. Visual experiences
There is a wide variety of visual experiences. Appearances range from "a transparent mist" to "absolutely solid." You may see only your relative's head and shoulders, or you may see his or her entire body. Some visual contacts occur in the bedroom, next to or at the foot of the bed. Others may happen anywhere – even in a car or aboard a plane. Typically he or she will be expressing love and well-being with a radiant smile. Loved ones virtually always appear healed and whole regardless of how they died. Verbal communication may take place, but not always.

### 6. Visions
An image of a deceased loved one may appear in a "picture" that is either two-dimensional or three-dimensional, like a hologram. It's like seeing a 35-millimeter slide or a movie suspended in the air. Visions are usually in radiant colors and may be seen externally, with your eyes open, or internally, in your mind. Communication may occur, especially during meditation.

## 7. Experiences while asleep

Sleep-state contact is much more vivid, intense, colorful and real in dreams. It is very common. Both one-way and two-way communications are typical. You usually feel your loved one is with you in person. These experiences are not jumbled, filled with symbols or fragmented like ordinary dreams.

## 8. Sleep-state encounters

Sleep-state encounters are similar to those that occur when you are awake. Your relative or friend can come to you more easily when you are relaxed, open and receptive, such as while you are in the alpha state or asleep.

## 9. Out-of-body communication

These may occur while you are asleep or in a meditative state. They are dramatic experiences during which you leave your body and visit your loved one at the place or level where he or she exists. These are extremely vivid, intense and real – some say more real than the physical world. The environments usually contain beautiful flowers, butterflies, colorful bushes and trees, radiant lighting and other aspects of nature – and are filled with happiness, love and joy.

## 10. Telephone calls

These may occur during sleep or when you are wide awake. You will hear a phone ringing, and if you answer it, your loved one will give you a short message. Two-way conversations are possible. His or her voice will usually be clear but may seem far away. You will probably not hear a disconnect sound or dial tone when the call is completed.

## 11. Physical phenomena

People who are bereaved often report receiving a wide variety of physical signs from their deceased relative or friend, such as lights blinking on and off; lights, radios, televisions, stereos and mechanical objects being turned on; or photographs, pictures and other items being turned over or moved.

## 12. Symbols and signs

People frequently ask a Higher Power, the universe, or their deceased loved one for a sign that he or she still exists. Many receive such a sign, though it may take some time to arrive. Occasionally these signs are so subtle they may be missed, or they may be discounted as mere "coincidences." Common signs include butterflies, rainbows, many species of birds and animals, flowers and a variety of inanimate objects such as coins and pictures.

*Bill Guggenheim and Judy Guggenheim: After-death communications researchers and authors.*

FATE August 1998

# DO WE CONTACT THE DEAD IN OUR DREAMS?
## Helen Solem

Can we believe that life goes on after death? Can our dreams provide the answer to this question?

I decided for myself years ago, not only because of my dreams but also because of conscious psychic experiences, that we can contact the dead. And through the years I have compiled a file of dreams from many people who believe they also have had contact with the dead. Astonishingly, if these reports are to be believed, the dead seem every bit as alive as you and I.

I decided to expand my collection of such dream contacts. I asked the editors of *Vital Signs,* the newsletter of the International Association for Near-Death Studies, to put such a request in their publication. (IANDS was founded by scholars and lay persons who are interested in the experiences of persons who have been pronounced clinically dead but who were resuscitated.)

I asked readers to report such dreams and to tell me if their dreams helped them in some way. I placed similar notices in the *Applied Psi Newsletter* and in the *Journal of Spiritual Frontiers Fellowship.* I received 47 responses detailing over 100 dreams from persons all around the country and from as far away as Japan. As I read through these remarkable accounts, I tried to identify the common, universal themes they contain.

It seems to me three main points stand out in these dreams: They assure us that death is not the end and that it is important to learn how to die; they also contain messages about what the next life is like.

Many of these dreams seem to represent genuine, personal contact with the dead. For example, one of my correspondents told about a curious dream she had in 1977 while recovering from her husband's death. One night, just after she had gone to bed, she felt someone tucking her in the way her husband used to do. Then she felt him bend down and kiss her, which he also always had done. The next morning at breakfast the dreamer asked her sister, with whom she was staying at the time, whether she had come into her room after she had gone to bed and tucked her in. The sister shook her head saying no, she had not. The experience seemed so real to the dreamer, and so precious, that all day long she kept remembering it and could hardly let herself believe it was true. So that evening when her sister came home from work she asked again if she'd come into her room the night before and tucked her in.

"No," the sister repeated. "Am I crazy or something? I told you this morning I didn't do that."

Many of these dreams contain information which the dreamer could have no way of knowing, thus further indicating their paranormal origin. Sometimes the message is not received in a dream but through a different type of psychic experience. Whether psychic experience or dream, they usually come just before or after a crisis as if to help the experiencer through it.

One such psychic experience was recounted to me by a woman who, at the age of 27, was expecting her fifth child. Life was hard for her family at that time. Her husband had been out of work for a while.

In this experience her brother, who had died in 1906 when he was 17 and who had been very close to the woman, appeared. She did not see him because he was behind her, but she knew his voice which she says was inaudible and thus must have sounded in her head.

8

He said, "You will have to choose. Will it be little Nancy or the new baby?" The whole experience was sharp and clear.

Without a moment's hesitation she answered, "I guess it will have to be little Nancy because the other children need me." Nancy was just a year and a half old.

When she woke the next morning and remembered her late-night experience she had no idea what it could mean. It was a busy house with small children to care for. Moreover, the doctor had put her to bed because of persistent bleeding. So, she had little time to analyze dreams.

About three weeks later little Nancy fell from the porch, struck her head a severe blow and died a short while later. Through that terrible time the mother somehow managed to retain her sanity, to protect the unborn baby and to stay alive herself. When reporting that experience now she says she believes it was given to her to help her through that calamitous time. However, she said, she still did not understand why there had to be a choice.

My first response was that maybe it was for a practical reason; her physical strength was not up to caring for a new baby and a toddler as well as the other children in the family. But I wondered why such a heartbreaking choice had to be hers. The answer came recently when I visited her.

She is now 90 years old and living near some of her family but in her own lovely little mobile home. We were talking about some of life's harder lessons and how difficult it is sometimes not only to like everyone but just to be decent to them.

She agreed and said, "Hard as some of these lessons are to learn, especially sometimes getting along with relatives (friends we can choose, but God gives us our relatives), they are nothing compared to the problem of sex, at least for me. When I was young I could hardly keep my hands off a man. I fear I pestered my poor husband near to distraction."

And like a light switching on, I realized why she was the one who had to choose between little Nancy or the new baby. The responsibility for bringing them into the world was hers.

One of my own first significant dreams of the dead was very similar. It made such a profound impression on me that it is responsible for my interest in this work and was undoubtedly preparing me for the death of a dear friend. Just before I woke that morning I saw my friend

9

in a dream. To get my attention he pinched me. He looked just as usual except that, as I remembered afterwards, I could see through him. He was downcast and sad; all he said was, "Goodbye." Then he reached out helplessly and seemed close to tears as he added, "I didn't make it, Helen."

As I sat on the edge of my bed wondering what that dream could mean, the radio came on with the seven o'clock news. One of the first things reported was that my friend's plane had gone down in the Columbia River the day before and sunk. No trace of my friend could be found.

One of the most impressive cases in my collection concerns a dreamer who told me of a series of contacts with the dead. One of her dreams contained information possibly known to the deceased person but not to the dreamer.

"Until my mother passed away in 1959," Gwen M. writes, "I don't specifically remember if I ever dreamed of anyone deceased or not. However, I was very distraught over my mother's death at the early age of 49. Many times after that she came to me in my dreams, especially when I was perplexed or disturbed about something."

The dreamer soon learned she could ask her mother's advice in these dreams and often did. Years later, having a family of her own and having seen her father retire, she dreamed one night of a room full of coffins. She screamed NO! NO! in the dream because, she said, she knew her father was going to die. Her mother then appeared in the dream and told her not to worry because she would be there to meet him.

A few days later her brother phoned her from Leesburg, Virginia and said their father was in the hospital. He was hemorrhaging and the doctors wanted to do vein bypass surgery. Her brother felt she should come right away. She hurried then to her father's bedside and knew that her dream was going to come true. The doctors insisted on an operation but could not give much hope of recovery.

She did her best to persuade her brother to refuse the operation, telling him about her dream. But he said they had to give their dad every possible chance to get well. She was certain he would die in surgery, but he did not. The operation didn't help, however, so a second was performed. Four days later her father passed away. But she didn't learn of his death from the doctors.

That morning early her mother appeared in her dream and announced, "It's all over." Gwen woke up then and looked at the clock beside her bed. It was just seven o'clock. Soon the hospital called to say that her father had passed away at 7:10 AM.

When she retired the night after the funeral she asked if she might talk to her dad to tell him how much she loved him. Later when she slept her mother came to her in a dream and told her that as soon as possible she would tell her father how she felt but that right now, seeing her, he might think he was still alive. The mother explained that it might be some while before her father could safely appear in a dream as it would take time for him to recover from his ordeal in the hospital. She then said, "My mother took me to see Dad. He was in a hospital, it seemed, and I was allowed to look in on him through a one-way glass."

About six months later, Gwen tells us, she finally met her father in a dream. In this dream she was standing at the rail on an excursion boat going down the bay as the family used to do on Sundays when she was growing up in Baltimore. As she stood there looking out over the water, her father walked up to her. He was looking much younger and well and strong again. He smiled and said he'd heard she wanted to talk to him.

Gwen explained that it wasn't until after she attended some Spiritual Frontiers Fellowship workshops that she realized she had been hanging onto her parents, had become so dependent on them that perhaps she was holding them back from their own spiritual progress. That very night she asked to see her mother one more time just to tell her she loved her and how much she appreciated all the good advice over the years. When she slept her mother appeared in a dream and said at once, "If you think you can make it now by yourself, I do have other things to do. But we'll be available if you need us."

It is very interesting how quickly and clearly the point is made in a dream. Also, the information given in a dream is often quite different from what one expects. The dream of the coffins is an example. Gwen M. wrote she'd been happily expecting a visit from her father when that dream came.

Carl Jung, the great Swiss psychologist, once said all the important events in our lives are first shown to us in dreams if we but paid attention.

Dr. Perriton Maxwell, who practiced medicine in New York City back at the turn of this century, wrote a marvelous account of how his patients' dreams helped him to diagnose their ills. In his engrossing book *A Third of Life*, Dr. Maxwell tells not only about restoring people to good health with the help of their own dreams but how contact with deceased persons brought comfort, peace and serenity back into the lives of bereaved patients. Maxwell learned that anyone – shopkeeper, housewife, nurse, attorney – can receive help from his dreaming self.

Oftentimes whole families can work together through their dreams to deal with family problems. The following is an example of such cooperation. It is from my own collection of dream contacts with the dead.

This dreamer told me that her brother-in-law, Dale, who had been working on the Alaska pipeline, was reported missing and presumed dead in June 1978. When the family first heard the news she and her husband, the missing man's brother, went to Alaska to try to locate him and then stayed to put his affairs in order. Dale had written glowing accounts of the far north and said he meant to stay there. He'd been investing his high wages carefully, he wrote, and had made a large down payment on a taxi service. The family soon learned that the former owner was still operating it and even tried to deceive them about Dale's having purchased it. Since his affairs were in a muddle and no trace of him could be found, they did what they could. They left the rest of the paperwork in the hands of a lawyer and sadly returned home.

My correspondent Doris Y., the sister-in-law, was a regular dreamer and felt certain someone in the family would learn through his dreams what all of them needed to know about Dale's disappearance. Doris' son-in-law was the first one to dream of Uncle Dale. He had just a glimpse of Dale in his dream, he reported, but he knew who it was; he said the feeling surrounding Dale was ominous; it seemed he was being beaten up. This caused the family to urge the police to continue their search.

Late fall the same year Dale disappeared, Doris had a clear dream of him. In her dream Dale was strolling towards her husband and her over a beautiful red carpet which seemed to be rolled out for the occasion. She said Dale looked well and much younger than when they had last seen him. He was dressed in his good suit, the one he wore when he was a Sunday school superintendent.

"Dale," she asked, "why have you done this to us?"

He looked away and then sort of shrugged and said, "You know how it is. Time just gets away from you."

When she told the family about her dream, they all agreed Dale was surely dead. The following summer (1979) the police reported they had found a skeleton in an old cabin near Valdez, Alaska, where Dale had often stayed when he went fishing. They reported that they had identified it as that of the missing man. They were unable to tell, they said, whether he had been deliberately injured or if his injuries had been accidental.

Some of you may ascribe dreams to "wish fulfillment" as Freud did. Others of you may dismiss them as the productions of overwrought imaginations. But some dream contacts with the dead provide the dreamer with such detailed and otherwise unknown information that they certainly cannot be classified as "normal" dreams.

For instance, a woman in Connecticut wrote that her father-in-law appeared to her in a dream the night after his funeral. He told her he had a bank savings book hidden in his bedroom and urged her to look for it. He said the account held $2800.

The next morning at breakfast when she told her husband about her dream he laughed and said, "That's ridiculous. Dad never could save a nickel."

So, the dreamer forgot about her dream. Then several weeks later her husband's stepmother phoned him to report that she'd discovered a bank savings book she'd known nothing about.

The son asked, "How much money did it have in it?" The reply was, "$2800."

And what is one to make of the following?

This helpful contact with the dead was reported to me by Lynn Jubishi who lives on Oshima Island adjacent to mainland Japan. At the time of his dream he had been suffering from an acute attack of tonsillitis. His throat was so raw it hurt even to swallow saliva. When he finally fell asleep on this night in 1979 a disciplined-looking military officer appeared to him. Somehow he "knew" that this was the stranger at whose tomb he and his four-year-old daughter had stopped for a moment while out for a walk a few days earlier. There were no flowers on this tomb as there were at most of the other tombs and the child had deliberately skipped over there. Together they had joined hands and silently offered a prayer for the peace of the soul of this forgotten person. The military man was now thanking him in the dream for his kindness at the tomb. He also asked if there was anything he might do for Jubishi in return. The dreamer pointed to his throat.

13

The other nodded curtly and said, "We'll take care of it."

Then the dreamer awoke and found his throat completely healed! He woke his wife to tell her about his remarkable dream and to ask for some food; he was famished because he had not eaten for several days.

Now comes the $64 question. Are these dreams really contacts with the dead? Or are they somehow manufactured by our dreaming minds?

The strongest argument against their being dramatizations from our unconscious minds is that the information they contain is often new and amazing.

Dreams are normally part and parcel of our emotional wellbeing. Some authorities believe that dream activity is simply a way of restoring emotional balance by ridding ourselves of the stress and tensions of the day. But when some clear, straightforward and heretofore unknown information comes through our dreams, it must be more than this.

Surely, we have been permitted access to this information for a good reason. It is possible such dreams come through the help of our own higher selves but when the dead appear in our dreams it seems logical to conclude that a mutual working relationship is manifesting.

Wherever dreams come from, it is important to remember they are a part of, an extension of, ourselves. The information given to us in our dreams, therefore, is a tool which we can use to help ourselves.

*Helen Solem: Writer, author and former board member of the Spiritual Frontiers Fellowship.*

FATE March 1984

# TYPES OF DREAM VISITS FROM THE DEAD
## Rosemary Ellen Guiley

After-death contact happens to many people who have lost loved ones. One of the most common – and powerful – mediums for contact is the dream. These are not "ordinary" dreams, full of jumbled images and symbols, but direct, intense contact that has a "real life," albeit otherworldly, feel. Dreams visits have a purpose, and they help the living come to closure and process their grief. They are *not* wish fulfillments.

The afterlife dreams we have today have a long history of similar experiences shared by our distant ancestors, and with other people all around the world. Relationships, especially within the family, continue after death, and ancestral spirits have the ability to interact in the lives of the living. Dream contact with the dead has a beneficial effect for both the living and the dead.

Since ancient times, dreams have been vehicles for viewing and visiting other realities beyond waking life. We can travel out-of-body and beyond time to have encounters with the dead and spiritual beings. Most of our dreams are more mundane – symbolic presentations of emotional states and conflicts from our waking life. Dream visits from the dead fall into that category of transcendent experience.

# Types of afterlife dreams

Perhaps you have had a significant dream involving contact or communication with the dead, or a vision of the afterlife. Many are lucid and seem like a real experience. There may be intense colors and an unusual atmosphere. All the physical senses are involved, including touch. Communication however, is telepathic. In most cases, the dead person has a renewed or refreshed appearance, and, if they died late in life, may appear as they looked when they were much younger.

Most afterlife dreams occur in several types:

## Farewells

Farewell dreams often involve people who are terminally ill. The dreamer dreams that the ill person comes to them to say good-bye as they leave the earth plane. Sometimes the farewell is within an intense, lucid dream. Other times, the person awakens – or thinks they awaken – and sees the departing person standing at the foot of the bed, or beside the bed. Their image is vivid and then fades away. The next day, the dreamer discovers that the person died the night before, or in the early morning hours.

Farewell encounter dreams also happen in cases of sudden and unexpected death, such as through accidents or violent ends. The dying person appears at a moment of extreme crisis or imminent death. In psychical research, these dreams are called "crisis apparitions." They usually appear to a loved one or friend with whom the dying person has close emotional ties. Sometimes their appearance reveals the manner of their death. Their clothing may look burned if they died in a fire, for example, or the figures may gesture to show their fatal wounds.

## Reassurances

In reassurance dreams, a dead person imparts the message that everything is all right. It is not unusual for the dead person to appear restored in health and youth and be radiant with happiness and energy. Reassurance dreams usually happen within a few days or weeks of a person's passing, when worry and grief are at a peak with the living – but they can also occur months or even years after someone has died.

## Life guidance

A dead person, not necessarily recently deceased, appears in a dream to impart advice, warnings, solutions to problems and creative ideas, or to bestow blessings of love and forgiveness. Their messages may be brief and couched in dream symbolism. Sometimes they have a long conversation with the dreamer. The meeting is realistic and may even involve touching and hugging. Sometimes the dreamer will not remember all the conversational details upon awakening but will nonetheless "know" what is to be done.

## Unfinished business

Few people die with full closure of every detail in their lives. Most of those concerns fall away with the transition to the afterlife. In some cases, however, there are important matters to be addressed, and the dead find a way to get their concerns through to the living. Such concerns usually involve their estates, burial requests, last wishes and so on.

## Proxy dreams

There are two types of proxy dreams. One is the appearance of a dead person on behalf of someone else who has died. The messenger is a person linked to the living recipient in some way. For reasons we may not understand, the dead – especially the newly dead – may not be able to communicate or be available, yet they desire to get a message across.

The second type of proxy dream is the appearance of a dead person in the dream of a family member or friend who will relay the message to the intended recipient.

One of the examples I have in *Dream Messages from the Afterlife: Visits from the Dead* (2017) concerns a deceased woman who appeared in dreams to her daughter-in-law, whom she asked to deliver a message to her son, the husband. The dream reunion was intensely realistic, with the sensation of physical contact. Communication was telepathic.

The daughter-in-law readily agreed to be the messenger but asked why her mother-in-law didn't tell her son directly. "I can't," she replied, "because of the way he dreams."

## Helping the dead

Our religions and spiritual faiths teach us that one of the best ways we can help the dead is through prayer, which sends tremendous spiritual energy between realms. On occasion, the dead need some extra help and may appear in dreams to reach out. If they died suddenly, they may be confused about where they are. In lucid dreams, a conversation can take place. Sometimes the dreamer awakens knowing they must pray for the dead.

In addition, there are other types of dreams involving the afterlife:

## Dreams that foretell death

Precognitive dreams warning of impending death have been documented since ancient times. People dream of the deaths of others and, rarely, of their own passing. The dead are often the messengers.

## Dreams of the dying and deathbed visions

Dreams and dream-like visions of the afterlife occur to individuals who are nearing death. Terminally ill patients may experience vivid contact with the dead and previews of the afterlife up to several weeks before they pass. Sometimes caregivers and family and friends participate in the experiences as well, by sharing visions and having their own corroborating dreams.

## Previews of the afterlife

Dreams take us to the edge of the afterlife, to places of transition and glimpses of what lies beyond. We have meetings with the dead, spiritual guides and helpers who explain the afterlife to us. These extraordinary dreams occur throughout life, often as part of spiritual awakenings and major transitions in life.

# Benefits of dream visits from the dead

Dream visits and messages from the dead can alleviate grief and facilitate closure and should be integrated into any counseling. Visitation dreams should be evaluated for both their symbolic content and their integrity as real events.

In addition, such dreams can help the living process beliefs and concerns about dying and the afterlife. Natural concerns and questions arise throughout life, as we ponder the meaning of why we are here, where we came from and where we are going when our time in done. Visitation dreams are direct experience, the most powerful way to acquire spiritual knowledge and wisdom.

*[Adapted from* Dream Messages from the Afterlife: Visits from the Dead *(2017) by Rosemary Ellen Guiley.]*

*Rosemary Ellen Guiley: Author, researcher and Executive Editor of FATE.*

# THE DEAD ARE ALIVE!
## Harold Sherman

Impressive and convincing as many near-death experiences are, some skeptical researchers still remind us that these seeming out-of-body projections do not necessarily prove life after death, since all those who have been pronounced clinically dead were not actually testifying from the afterlife.

For this reason, in my book *The Dead Are Alive*, I did not include any of the case histories of such near-death experiences in my files; instead I presented evidence from and about those who have actually departed this life. Since my book was published I have received an increasing number of case histories involving spirit return from men and women who, no longer afraid of ridicule, are willing to testify to bring comfort and hope to those persons who have lost loved ones or are themselves facing death.

The kind of evidence strongly suggesting life after death that I am presenting can never be demonstrated in a scientific laboratory.

But neither can it be faked. These happenings were spontaneous and unexpected and occurred when the percipients were awake. The subjects report occasions when their departed loved ones have fully materialized in daylight as well as in dark and have communicated by actual voice as well as in a "feeling" or by telepathy. In some cases they have touched, embraced and even kissed the living!

One of the most remarkable cases, chosen from our ESP Research Associates Foundation files in Little Rock, Arkansas, is related by Nancy F. from Virginia who has asked that I not reveal her full name and identity because some of her friends and relatives would not approve:

> Dear Mr. Sherman: I have just read your book You Live After Death. I never really believed that people could make contact with loved ones in another world – until my husband died on April 23, 1979.
>
> In August of 1979 I was lying in bed and the kids were asleep; it was after 12 at night.
>
> I heard my door, which was securely locked, open and I saw my husband come through the door and sit down in a chair beside my bed. Then he reached down and kissed me and I saw and felt the ring which I had left on him in the coffin.
>
> He looked like he did when he was well. He had his hair and it was black... and he had no scars on his head and face.
>
> Before he died – he had cancer – they had removed his tongue, part of his face, his neck, and he had no hair. His head had come loose from his shoulders because his body had rejected the skin grafts... and he had lots of sores on his head and face. But now his face looked perfect.

If we accept Nancy's experience as genuine – and I personally do not doubt it – then it has to be reassuring to many who have lost loved ones as the result of some debilitating disease or bad accident to know that they have left all suffering and disfigurement behind on entering the next life.

Nancy goes on to write:

*There have been several times when I have wakened during the night and felt my husband's presence. I have thought I saw him standing in the doorway, watching over me.*

*My son, who is 12 years old, said he woke up one night and saw his father standing over his bed, smiling at him.*

*The last time he appeared to me was when I was awake a few weeks ago and my grandmother, who has been dead for 28 years, was standing with him beside the bed. This surprised me because my husband never met my grandmother. She had been dead for five years before I even met my husband. Both of them told me things I had been worrying about were going to be better in a little while.*

*I know these visitations were not dreams. My son wasn't dreaming when he also saw his father who was right there looking after him as he used to do in life.*

*So, you can understand, Mr. Sherman, that I have reason – not to believe – but to know that people survive death.*

The heart-touching case of William Ballyn of North Vancouver, British Columbia, which came to me recently has the ring of truth to it:

*Dear Mr. Sherman: It is now just two-and-a-half years since the deep emotional experience which I have finally decided to report to you. First, I should tell you that I am living in my son's home; he is a bachelor and an architect.*

*I sleep in a bedroom on the ground floor which overlooks the back garden. This room was occupied by my dear wife and myself (before she died). She was an invalid and I gave her day and night care for four years. The last two she was in a wheelchair and was badly confused.*

*Finally, my son suggested that his mother be sent to an extended care unit where she was looked after for three more years.*

*In April 1978 I had just visited her the day before, when the doctor called me at 4 AM to tell me of her passing. Her body was cremated and the ashes were sent to me by the crematorium.*

*What I am now to report happened on Monday, April 17, 1978, at approximately 4:30 AM. I had retired at about 11 PM and was reading your book* You Live After Death, *which I often refer to for the comfort it brings me. The next thing I was aware of, I was sitting on the side of the bed facing the garden window and the love seat in front of it.*

*Lying on this small sofa was my darling wife Thelma.*

*She had her legs drawn up and was partially turned toward the window, so I could not clearly see her face. She appeared to be dressed in a sort of nebulous garment of a light color, reaching to her midcalf, similar to a negligee.*

*I rushed over to her, exclaiming, "Sweetheart! Oh, my darling! I have you here!" at the same time turning her towards me.*

*Her hair was thick, luxuriant, long and black, and it cascaded over her shoulders as I turned her. She looked at me and her face was beautiful to behold – young and radiant – as when she was 17! (She was 68 at the time of her death.) Her eyes were full of love but she looked at me without speaking. "Can you walk, my darling?" I asked and turned her limbs toward the floor.*

*She smiled and swung her legs out as if to rise. I swept her into my arms, holding her closely... and pounded the floor with my bare feet, calling my son Christopher who slept in the basement room below. I had forgotten that he had remained in town over the weekend and I kept calling, "Christopher, Christopher, I have Mom here. Come quickly."*

*In my state of ecstasy, not realizing that Christopher was not home, I kept calling and thumping. "Christopher! Come quickly, I have dear Mom here." My wife felt real, warm and solid in my arms and we gazed at each other. Realizing now that my son was not at home, I also became conscious that my darling wife seemed to be shrinking. I spoke to her, saying, "Oh, darling, I have you here with me!"*

*She looked at me with an expression of utmost love and said very softly, "No, Daddy, I died."*

*"No, darling," I replied, holding her closely. "I have you here with me again."*

*She said once more, "No, Daddy, I died."*

*The tone of her voice was that of a mother explaining with great tenderness to a child. Nothing more was said by my wife as she kept becoming less and less in my arms, with me frantically calling, "No, no! Don't leave me."*

*Then she was gone, and I found myself sitting on the side of the bed again, shaken and completely distraught, looking at my bedside clock. It was 4:30 AM and a faint dawn was coming up. This is my complete experience, word for word, exactly as it happened to me over two-and-a-half years ago – as clear to me now as when it occurred. The experience was utterly real.*

Mrs. J. W. Baker of Indianapolis, Indiana, tells about the two times she feels her late husband contacted her:

*My husband died in June 1969 of a heart attack. I was in Minnesota at our cabin at the time. I had talked to him on a Sunday night and the last thing he said to me was "I love you." I said, "I love you, too."*

*The next morning, I got the call saying he was gone. Nerve alone carried me through the next few days but after the funeral when I was alone I really went to pieces. Worst of all, I lost all faith. I was so very bitter, and I kept thinking, "How do I know there's a heaven? How do I know he's not just lying in the ground and I'll never see him again?"*

*Then I would pray for faith to believe I'd see him again. I prayed for something – anything – to let me know he was still going on. I hadn't been able to eat or sleep; I had lost almost 35 pounds in less than two months and I knew I'd have to do something.*

*One morning I made up my mind I'd work so hard that I'd be able to sleep when night came. So I cut grass; I raked; I pulled weeds; and when night came I dragged myself into the house, bathed, said my prayers, fell into bed and went right to sleep.*

*I don't know how long I had slept – probably two or three hours – when I wakened. I turned toward the window and there was the most beautiful full moon. I lay there, my mind a blank, for perhaps 20 minutes. Then I turned away, closed my eyes and was almost asleep but not all the way. I remember thinking that I wished I could get over the last lump and go back to sleep.*

*Suddenly my husband's arms were around me. He kissed me twice very hard. Frantically I patted his face. Then he said something to me, but I cannot recall what it was. I smiled so happily and instantly was fast asleep and slept till morning.*

*About 10 days later, on a Saturday morning, I went into our bedroom and lay down. I was facing the closet doors. Again, my mind was a blank – just numb – my eyes were closed, and I was almost asleep when I heard three loud knocks. My eyes flew open and there against the closet doors, in a space of about 18 square inches, I saw my husband from his shoulders up. He had his hand raised in a wave and was smiling happily at me. I smiled back and closed my eyes. Then I thought, "You didn't wave back." I opened my eyes again but there was nothing there. Instantly I was asleep - the sleep I needed so much.*

*Mr. Sherman, I have told this to friends and relatives. A few have believed this happened; others I know have thought I was dreaming or hallucinating, but I was not. I wrote these things down so I would not forget any details.*

*When they happened I thought, "How wonderful. Now he can come to me often." But never again! Now I realize this was the answer to my prayers. Now I know he is still going on and I will be with him again. I know that God or some Higher Power heard my prayers, felt compassion for my despair and let these things happen. My husband was so protective toward me and I know the happy smile on his face was to assure me, in the only way he could, that everything was fine and my fears were groundless.*

*One other thing, when I saw him that morning it seemed as though he was behind a very sheer white curtain. Everything I have written is exactly as it happened. I do not want one false word to cloud this wonderful memory.*

So often husbands, or wives particularly, are visited by departed loved ones in the night after they have retired, when their minds are at rest and more receptive, free from the day's conflicting demands.

Such a case was reported to us by Gloria Davis of Knoxville, Tennessee:

*My husband died almost two years ago. We were on our way home, on an air evacuation plane, from Camp Zarna, Japan, on May 25, 1970. He died between Japan and California.*

*I was expecting our baby. We were married only three months and I was nearly three months pregnant – a blessing for both of us. Our baby was born on October 26, 1970, and it was maybe two or three months later that my husband, Gene, came to see me.*

*I thought I was asleep but I wasn't. I had just gotten in bed and was thinking of how proud Gene would have been. I heard someone say, "I am proud, Gloria, very proud of our son."*

*I turned and Gene was there! He came and sat on the edge of the bed next to me. We sat there for a while staring at our newborn son before Gene started talking again. He said he had seen me at his grave the day before. I had started to cry so he left.*

*Gene told me it was very hard for him to maintain this state so he'd have to leave me soon and try again someday. He blew me a kiss and left through the door he had entered.*

*When I realized that I was really awake and sitting up, I ran into the next room where my girlfriend was sleeping and scared the immortal hell out of her. We both started crying and then I started smiling. Susie thought I was crazy. I was just so glad that Gene had come home one more time.*

*That's my story and now I believe in the powers of ESP. I had always thought it was silly and people who believed in it were crazy. Since then I have had visions and dreams of things and they have come true. I've been places I've never been before and felt I had. Life is wonderful.*

Yes, life seems wonderful to those who have had experiences like Gloria's. But there are many who long to contact departed loved ones who have not been able to do so. Just why this does not happen, why conditions, whatever they need be, have not permitted these spirit manifestations, no one yet knows. It is always possible that the spirits of loved ones are present but those whom they are trying to contact are not sufficiently endowed psychically to sense or see them. However, more and more people who have never had any psychic awareness before are having these experiences. This suggests that the phenomenon may be a form of energy that has to be generated before these spirit entities can manifest. There have been consistent reports that when the energy that enables spirits to appear runs out, their forms dissolve and disappear back into the next dimension. This leads to the possible conclusion that the difference between dimensions of existence can be a matter of frequency.

Doris McClure Humphrey of Rockville, Maryland, sent me the following letter:

*Dear Mr. Sherman: For a long time I've wanted to write to you but have delayed doing so because it's hard to find the right words to describe psychic experiences. Two years ago I bought a secondhand battered (falling apart) copy of* You Live After Death. *Apparently it had been read to shreds but fortunately the book had all its pages. I was glad to find the book is still in print so I could get a new copy. Now I am halfway through your new book* The Dead Are Alive *and want to tell you about two contacts (it seemed to me) with my beloved father Wallace A. McClure who died in October 1978 at the age of 82.*

*My father and I were very close in interests and in sympathy. He had heart trouble the last 20 years of his life so I was not unprepared when the phone call came telling me my father had died. The last year or so of his life Daddy would phone me at least once a week, sometimes twice (we were 500 miles apart). But, as I said, we were very close in our thoughts. We occasionally shared ESP experiences.*

*One time I picked up the phone to call my father and before I could dial he was on the line. "Good evening," he said. He had called me at exactly the same time. "Remember, we are always in touch," he said. So the trip to Ohio and the funeral were not quite as devastating as they might have been because I knew my father and I would always be in touch.*

*Now I want to tell you of the two experiences I have had; some people would call them lucid dreams – the kind of dreams which you feel are more than dreams.*

*These two times my father is standing beside my bed and it's early in the morning, time to get up, and the sunlight is streaming into the room. I tell myself it's a dream and if I reach out to touch my father he won't really be there. Remember, this not only happened once, but twice. I reached out and touched him and I felt the shoulder of his gray suit.*

*After I woke up, if I actually had been asleep, I could still feel the woolen material under my fingertips.*

*In these contacts with my father I always say, "Daddy, are you all right?" And he says, "Of course I'm all right."*

*My father appears to be about 50 years old, vigorous and healthy. He looks at me with such kindness and love. Until now I haven't told anyone about what has happened. But I know it's all right to tell you.*

Katie Thompson, a longtime friend of ours here in Mountain View, Arkansas lost her husband, Louis, by death and moved to Red Bluff, California to live. She wrote recently:

*I would like to think that the experience I had could be of comfort to someone. I have always believed that our spirit lives on. But seeing Louis' spirit was a first sighting. I look for more.*

*It happened one night about a year ago. I was feeling very lonely. As I was getting into bed I cried out loud, "Oh, God, I wish I could see Louis once more."*

*I think I fell asleep. Then I woke up and saw Louis standing at the foot of my bed. His features and body line were clear but everything about him was gray. I rose quickly and reached out my arms toward him. Just then I heard Louis' voice call "Mother" very urgently and he disappeared.*

*I lay back down with a dreadful pain in my heart. I told myself it was because I had gotten up so quickly.*

*Well, was it a dream? I thought it over and decided that Louis' call meant that I was still needed here. What do you think?*

There is no set answer to such a question. It is possible that there is meaning behind every spirit return but that meaning is not always clearly indicated or interpreted. For some inexplicable reason, these spontaneous manifestations are usually a once-in-a-lifetime event for most persons.

It seems that once our departed loved ones have succeeded in demonstrating that they have survived death they go on about the business of existing in the next dimension, knowing their dear ones will join them one day.

*Harold Sherman (1898-1987): Prominent psychical researcher, author and lecturer.*

FATE December 1983

# LAST NIGHT I DREAMED OF RUTH
## Robert Weinstein

Last night I saw Ruth. She suddenly and unexpectedly returned to me in my dream.

My wife Ruth has been dead for over 25 years. Since the day she died I have not been able to picture her face at any time, asleep or awake. Nor have I been able to recall in picture form any part of our life together. Now, for the first time, she reappeared in my dream.

Of course, what happened that long ago, March 14, 1957, when Ruth died, was that her cancer had been so prolonged and so horrible that my mind shut down, blocking out all memory of her. I could talk about her and remember incidents from our life together, but I could not picture her. I could stare at her photograph but when I turned away I could not see again in my mind's eye her sweet pretty face.

When the children were very young, Sari, three, and Larry, seven, and spoke of their departed mother, I felt that all the things they remembered had not happened to us but rather to some other family we had known in the past. There was a detachment or gap between the life we had lived together and what remained after she was gone.

Now, as a sort of distant, foggy memory, I recall that our children grew up, left home and were well launched on their own successful careers and lives. A generation after she died, Ruth became a grandmother and I a grandfather, when our daughter Sari had a baby girl, Jodi.

Yet, in my dream, when Ruth at last appeared to me on the 25th anniversary of her death, she was again a pretty young girl as she was when I first met her. I have no explanation for how this was possible. Where had the memories been all those years? Locked in some dark corner or recess of my mind, hidden beyond my powers to call them out. Perhaps something triggered my memory, jolted my cerebral circuits, causing her image to burst forth in freshness and clarity, bridging the years.

I do not believe in the supernatural or ghosts or even in life after death or anything else that defies natural law, but I must admit that sometimes things happen that cast some doubt on my beliefs. All I am saying now is that something happened in my brain during my sleep. I am the first to deny that any sort of miracle occurred or that there is no rational explanation for what happens when we are asleep. I am simply saying that I saw Ruth in my dream and she spoke to me in my dream; we communicated and when 1 awoke I recalled everything that had transpired in my dream.

I am relating this as simply as I can. I am not trying to interpret my dream or look for hidden meanings. I am not trying to make the dream more significant than it was. I am just saying that my mind encountered some sort of inner vision. I leave it to the analysts to make whatever interpretations they wish. I deal only in hard reality.

I can't prove any of what I am writing down. To a tough mind like mine, this is disturbing.

Some people may think what happened was some sort of love story or something equally silly. That can't be. I am an old man, admittedly gruff and certainly not sentimental or soft in any way. I was in business for over 50 years and I pride myself on being a realist. I dealt in hard, practical matters. The years molded me into the kind of man I am. I am not denying that the dream happened; I am just trying to put it in its proper perspective, to give it proper value. I do not want the dream to appear to be anything more than it actually was, some kind of mental aberration that can happen when you are asleep and your defenses are down.

Perhaps if a brainwave recorder or some such device had been connected to my head, the machine might have recorded some unusual activity. Perhaps someday someone will invent a "black box" which will record the voltage, amperage and frequencies of the brain's activity while we sleep and make it possible to play back the dream on a screen at a later date. But there goes my practical mind, trying to convert fantasies into reality, into products. But I assure you the dream happened. It is as real to me as the sun, the skies, the trees.

Dreams are commonplace. 1 frequently have vivid, memorable dreams, sometimes in color. I trained my mind years ago to remember my dreams by the simple expedient of repeating over and over again before I dropped off to sleep, "I will remember my dreams. I will remember my dreams." I had read this method of remembering dreams in a scientific book somewhere. After a while it became second nature for me to recall my dreams and it was not necessary to make any special effort to do so. This idea did not work all the time, I hasten to add, but it worked enough times to satisfy me that the brain can and does retain dreams. Probably every dream is recorded somewhere in the brain, like data entered into a computer, to lie dormant just like other memories, until triggered into recall by something, sometime.

I also have nightmares about my experiences in the 20th Air Force during World War II, specifically the 313th Wing based on Tinian in the Marianas. I am not unduly disturbed by these wild dreams. I accept them with a sort of wry humor. I surely do not place any special significance on them. I have been assured at the Veterans Administration Hospital that nightmares are quite common to war veterans.

Sometimes in the past I have waked with pounding heart and racing pulse, shaking and afraid, but I have shrugged off these violent dreams by telling myself, "It was only a nightmare. What I dreamed about happened a long time ago and cannot harm me now."

Yet my dream of Ruth had a special bizarre, eerie quality which disturbed and puzzled me greatly. It was something Ruth said to me in the dream. I could not grasp the meaning of her words. I see now that I have fallen into the trap of accepting the dream as reality. Does a dream have a real existence? Was I being warned? Has something already been decided, somewhere, events beyond my ability to comprehend? Is there a time element in dreams? I do not know if there is a serious message in the dreams, especially in what Ruth told me at the very end, in her last words.

In my dream Ruth was there in front of me as if she had always been there. She did not suddenly appear or come into view or approach gradually. I cannot explain what happened – dreams are a special weird world of their own and must be accepted on their own terms. Ruth was just there as if it were the most natural thing in the world, despite the many years that had elapsed since she died. In the dream I accepted her appearance calmly and naturally, as if I had expected her. She was there; I was there. There was no setting; we were not in any place. There were just the two of us in a world void of everything else.

At the time of her death Ruth had wasted away. The bones of her face and body had protruded horribly, pushing against the sallow skin. My poor Ruth was not a pretty sight as she lay unconscious most of the time during the latter stages of the disease because of the massive dosages of morphine that were administered by the nurse who tended her during the day or injected by me the rest of the time.

I still remember with horror how black and blue Ruth's arms and body were from the frequent stabbings of the hypodermic needle. I cannot picture them but the horror is still there. Her body was so wasted that sometimes it was difficult to find a place that was suitable for injection.

But in my dream Ruth was in the full bloom of young womanhood, healthy, vivacious, brimming with personality and vitality, exactly as she had been in the earlier days of our marriage. I would say that she appeared to be in her late 20s or early 30s in the dream, although at the time of her death she was 45.

Now here is a curious thing: I was my present self, a crusty old man of 71 years, perhaps still alert but nevertheless an old man. I do not know how this could be but Ruth instantly recognized me as if I had not aged. Even before she spoke Ruth kissed me. I do not remember how she was dressed but it seems to me it was in something simple. In life Ruth always liked purple because it was becoming to her and because I like it. In the dream I was not cognizant of color of any kind. I think now that there had to be colors in the dream, but I was not aware of them.

Ruth simply leaned forward, smiled faintly and brushed my lips with hers. It was not a passionate or long kiss but simply a touching of her parted lips against mine. I was passive, my eyes open in apparent surprise. A dream is remarkable in that the sleeping person sees and hears and experiences all that transpires although his eyes are closed. No words are spoken aloud and whatever he thinks is happening is really only in his own mind.

It did occur to me that there was no smell of perfume. In life Ruth always used a touch of some perfume that gave me pleasure. We had many a laugh over that and she thought I was rather silly over that perfume. In the dream there was no perfume. Odd that such an integral part of her personality should be missing. Or is there no sense of smell in dreams? There is so much I do not know.

After the kiss Ruth and I gazed at each other for a moment. At least it seemed like only a moment but in dreams the time factor varies. Perhaps an hour passed, perhaps a split second. I am giving my best recollection. It is difficult to be precise about a dream.

My expression was of amazement and wonder. Ruth wore an amused, knowing, delighted smile, like someone who knows she has surprised you and is getting great pleasure out of your amazement. My mind, in the dream, was completely blank for a time after the kiss.

You would think that I would have had a thousand questions, that my astonishment would find expression. After all, many years had elapsed. But I was not in control of my senses and dreams do not follow any rational pattern. There is an air of acceptance in dreams. What is happening seems perfectly reasonable.

I spoke first, after l know not how much time had passed. It was as if we had met in an ordinary way in real life.

I said, "Ruth!" in a surprised and inquisitive tone, indicating that Ruth's appearance was unexpected but still accepted by me. It seemed to me that Ruth was pleased by the surprise on my face, for she smiled her charming smile a bit more broadly, just as she had in real life whenever she prepared a surprise for me. That had been a great delight of mine, the many little surprises my Ruth had prepared for me. She did not respond immediately to my calling out her name.

It occurred to me that Ruth showed no shock or disappointment at my age and appearance. Remember, I was only 45 at the time she was stricken. Certainly, I was then of a more youthful appearance than I am now. Instead, Ruth seemed to accept my balding head, my craggy face, all the signs of age that had inevitably appeared.

She stood silently before me, graceful and slim as she had always been. I suppose I could not dream of her differently. Certainly, if I had any choice, I would have wanted her to appear just as she appeared in my dream. I want to add that, in this dream, there were no wraithlike forms, no nebulous misty shapes, no bloodcurdling sounds. Ruth was as she had been in her youth and I was as I am now. No daily, ordinary things were included; nothing else existed in that vacuum of a dream but Ruth and me.

I last heard Ruth speak over 25 years ago; yet, when she spoke for the first time in the dream, her voice was instantly recognizable. It had the same tone, expression and timbre as long ago. It was curious that I was taking part in the dream and yet, observing clinically all that happened, I was a part of the dream and at the same time detached.

I would have recognized Ruth's voice even if I had not seen her. She spoke softly, as always, and I had no difficulty understanding her. I cannot say I heard her because it is obvious there was no actual voice. Nevertheless, I heard her words, "Bob, you did a wonderful job with the children." An ordinary everyday statement made during a remarkable dream.

I must interject here what I think was a small oddity in the incident. I must include it because it happened, but it had no place in the dream, no connection with what was happening. Perhaps it did not even make sense. But in dreams we have no control; the dream controls us.

One time in a deep sleep I dreamed I was walking along a road and met some people I knew. "What are you doing here?" one asked. "You are far from home."

I replied, "I am not far from home. I am asleep in my own bed. This is only a dream."

And so in this dream of Ruth I must include the extraneous thought I had in my dream although I do not see what it has to do with what was happening. It flashed through my mind that if only I had a tape recorder I could capture Ruth's voice on tape. What a curious, erroneous thought to have in a dream. There were, of course, no real voices. A tape would have been blank. Perhaps subconsciously I wanted to capture and hold part of the dream. The thought about the tape recorder flashed through my mind and promptly disappeared. I really do not understand the workings of the mind.

I spoke to Ruth again. My voice was not the gruff harsh voice I now have but held the tender, loving tone I had always used with her. "The children were so young when you died, Ruth," I said. "I didn't know what to do. I did the best I could. Your cousin Helen offered to take the kids, but I knew you wouldn't want me to give them up."

Ruth showed no shock when I said she had died. She replied in her silken voice, "I helped you as much as I could. I was always there when you really needed me."

"Were you?" I asked. "I sometimes felt that something from outside was helping me as I muddled through the meals, the laundry, the kids' schooling, all the problems I had, besides my business problems. Oh, I sold our house after the kids had graduated college and left."

"Yes," Ruth said, smiling serenely, "I know."

I added, "Sometimes I thought I was being helped by my mother or father. I kept getting lucky breaks whenever disaster threatened. The children were so healthy and cooperative and loving. They did so well, even when I was all broken up with grief. I couldn't understand how I was managing to get along."

Ruth smiled. "I know, "she said again.

I went on, "I didn't ever think it was your help I was getting because something happened to my mind after you went away. I couldn't picture you or remember much about you. The doctor said the shock of your death had been too much for me. Blanking out my memory was how my mind protected itself. Otherwise I'd have gone crazy."

"Yes, I know," Ruth said, nodding slightly in her familiar way. "I understood. I couldn't do everything I wanted to do for the children and you, but I did all I could."

I nodded. "I sent the kids through college," I said. "They did well. They got degrees. We prospered too because the business went well. There was always enough money. Was that you, Ruth, who guided me, showed me the way?"

"Not all the time," Ruth replied. "I could do only so much. There are rules, there are limits. Mostly I tried to put thoughts in your head. You did the rest."

"Was that how it happened?" I wondered.

Ruth nodded and said, "Now I must go. There is one more thing that I must tell you. That is what I really came to say."

In the dream I stood mute as Ruth told me the reason she had come back to me in my dream. Then she was gone. She did not fade away in a puff of swirling smoke but was suddenly gone – just not there anymore.

In the instant that she was gone, I awoke. It was morning. I recalled everything in all the detail I have written down. There is no question in my mind that the dream happened and that in the dream we kissed and spoke as I have recorded here.

But now a lot of questions come to my mind. Why didn't I tell Ruth that I have always loved her and love her still? Why didn't I ask if she would come to me again in future dreams? How did my mind reconstruct her face and body so that she was beautiful again?

Also, I wonder what the effect of the dream will be. Am I now released from the grip of the emptiness, the void, the blankness that have enveloped me since her death? Is death not final after all?

I must consider also what Ruth said she had really come back to tell me, what she said was the real purpose of her nocturnal visit.

Before she disappeared, she whispered softly, "You will be with me soon."

Was this all a foolish dream? Or have I received a genuine message from the next world?

FATE April 1986

# MY FRIEND THERE WAS YOU
## Bette Goodson

All my life I have been different. Even in my own family, I don't fit in. I am very drawn to the mystical, the mysterious and the supernatural, yet I was born into a family that considers all this to be either witchcraft or just plain crazy.

I have been on an intense spiritual path for many years and have been involved in several organizations. It has been stimulating, exhilarating, enlightening and fun. I have met some wonderful and interesting people.

## I meet Charlie
I teach a ladies' exercise class. One evening a slightly older lady attended. She was friendly and enthusiastic, but I felt she was much too sophisticated for my class. I teach low-impact aerobics with some yoga, toning and weights included. However, she joined in wholeheartedly and was the life of the class.

After the first class, Charlie (her nickname) stayed to ask if I knew yoga. I admitted that I did, even though I was forbidden to talk about yoga at work because of the "religious connotations." We spent an hour getting acquainted and finding out that we were birds of a feather. We fit!

Charlie became my best friend, and I like to think I became at least one of hers. We got together to study Edgar Cayce's *Search for God* books and we attended passion plays. I introduced her to my *A Course in Miracles* group and took her to several haunted house rescue missions. We went to Yogaville, Sri Swami Satchidananda's ashram in Buckingham, Virginia, several times. I introduced her to Swami Satchidananda and she responded to his universal love wholeheartedly. I will never forget the look of pure joy on her face when he blessed her favorite necklace. I was happy to be a part of that moment.

## My friendship with Charlie

Charlie was just like me. She could be deeply spiritual one minute and just a tad bawdy the next. She was delightfully eccentric and outspoken. She loved me with all her heart. No matter what, she was on my side all the way and just would not concede that I had any faults whatsoever.

Charlie was even a little stubborn. After exercise class, she and some of the ladies used the spa. Charlie liked all the lights off with just a ribbon of light under the door. The ladies complained that they felt uncomfortable. I tried everything to get her to leave the sliding switch on at least halfway, but to no avail. I even put up a sign saying that it was for safety purposes, but she said there was plenty of light.

She was also very frugal, so when she suddenly departed on a two-week, very expensive cruise, I was surprised and somewhat incredulous that she would leave her aged mother for so long. That was completely out of character for her. Before she left, she returned everything that she had borrowed from people saying that she wanted to get everything back where it belonged. She had a big yard sale and sold lots of things. She had all her business and funeral arrangements taken care of and signed a living will.

Upon her return, we went out for our Friday night Chinese dinner and I asked how her mother had done without her. She replied, "Just fine, which I'm glad to know in case anything should happen to me." She also said three times that she had a new philosophy and she wanted me to listen up: "Yesterday is gone and tomorrow may never get here, so make today count."

On Monday, she came to class, and because it was crowded, said she thought she would just get into the spa. I thought she seemed subdued or tired and I asked if she was all right. After class, she left hurriedly and again, I asked if she was okay. She assured me that she was but had a meeting and that we would talk the next day.

## Charlie passes

During the night, Charlie fell down her stairs and died. My daughter came to deliver the bad news that Charlie's mother had just found her that morning. I was devastated. I said, "I know if there is any way she can get back to tell me that she is okay, she will."

My daughter added, "How long has that angel been on your window?" I saw, on the window I had cleaned the day before, a bug splatter that made a perfect angel. It was about five inches tall and was so detailed I could see the part in her hair.

After the next exercise class, I was crying when I took down the sign about the lights. I turned out all the lights and was the last person to leave the building. The next morning, my daughter was the first one in the building and the lights in the spa room were on halfway.

Charlie, you were here.

Everything was an adventure to Charlie, and she could make anything fun. We had some of our best laughs when we got lost or when she got pulled over for speeding. She drove like a maniac, and because she scared me to death, I insisted upon driving 99 percent of the time. At her funeral, the minister told a story of Charlie and her family being in a small boat on Lake Michigan when a storm came up. Everyone was frightened except Charlie, who was in the bow of the boat riding the waves and having an adventure. At that exact moment in the minister's story, a big wind came from nowhere and nearly blew the funeral tarp away. We all said, "There's Charlie," and had a big laugh.

## The message

Several months later, I was at a meditation circle group. I had not spoken about Charlie that day, and my host's wife had never met her nor discussed her passing with me. At the close of the circle, Mary started writing. She said, "I have no idea what this means, but this is what I got."

The message said, "We are here now and it is light ahead. When death came I just kept on keeping on, going on, and all is well now. I found my way down a flight of stairs and stepped into the waters."

We all sat staring blankly for a moment, and I said, "That's Charlie."

I miss my friend. I had her for only a year and a half, but we got a lot of living in. She filled a void in my life and nothing is quite as much fun without her.

I don't really believe that her death was an accident because I feel that on the soul level she knew. I believe she took the cruise in order to give all who loved her the experience of separation before the final leaving. I believe that last night in exercise class, her aura and life force had started to diminish, and I sensed it. Never before had I felt compelled to ask if she was all right.

## I dream of Charlie

I appreciate the ways Charlie has shown me that she is still in my life. She has come as a perfect orb of light in my bedroom and she has come in my dreams. In one, I was laughing as I walked along behind her and another lady. She stopped and looked around with a twinkle in her eye and said, "What are you laughing about?"

I said, "I'm laughing about you. I know you're dead because we buried you. I just don't know how you're doing this." She gave me a wink and a hug and said, "Don't worry about how I'm doing it. Just have a good time, okay?"

Yes, she is still my soul friend. I am open to receiving whatever she can share with me from the other side. I hope we will meet again someday. She gave me the opportunity to share my interests and introduce her to people and places that I loved. She helped me believe in myself and she helped me to find my niche. Looking back, I know that she was a very enlightened soul who gave much more than she got. Why don't we recognize these souls as we go about our daily lives? So, Charlie, wherever you are, you go, girl, and enjoy your grand adventure. Make it count!

*Bette Goodson: Homemaker whose passions are family, gardening, reading, historical figures and her exercise class.*

FATE November-December 2011

# FATHER'S SPIRIT FORESAW CRISIS
## Judy Arriola

The early morning air on October 14, 1975, was bitingly cool and by 3 AM Jack Frost had made his famous ritual paintings on the windows in Sterling, Colorado where I lived.

I had just arrived home, dog-tired from a hard night's work at the Longhorn Saloon. It was one of those nights when one of my bartenders hadn't shown up for work and after doing a double-duty shift, I didn't bother with my usual nightly shower. Letting my clothes drop by the bed, I gratefully crawled beneath the covers. It didn't take me long to doze off – and into troubled sleep.

As I slept, I felt as if everything were floating in slow motion as I watched a silver-gray coffin lined with blue satin rotate in and out of a velvet darkness. I could feel myself striving hard to reach it, knowing someone I loved was in there. I wanted desperately to see who was inside of it. But just as I would get nearly close enough, a crowd of nondescript people would gather about it, keeping me from seeing whom the casket contained.

Once in my dream, when I broke through the crowd and was able to see inside death's bed, the coffin disappeared, and my father's face replaced it. He was smiling with peace and contentment. At that point I woke up drenched with perspiration.

The first time I had this dream I thought it was because I was overtired. But it kept returning nightly. For two weeks I dreamed the exact same dream, no matter whether I was extremely tired or not.

I remember the first Wednesday in November, the fifth, because I did my monthly books and inventory on that day. At 2 PM the phone rang. My barmaid Jerrie yelled that it was for me. Before I touched the phone, I instinctively knew it was my mother and I knew what her message would be.

In between her broken sobbing she told me Dad had had a severe stroke and wasn't expected to live.

After making the necessary arrangements with my assistant manager Nancy, I left for Iowa City a few hours later. I drove into the Veteran's Administration Hospital's parking lot 12 hours after that. There, in the emergency room, I found my mother, Lillian, my younger brother, Travis, 30, and Randy, my older brother, 41. As I looked into my family's faces, concern and fear overrode my weariness.

Mother rose from her chair with her arms outstretched. Hugging me, she broke down. Between her sobs she poured out, "Oh-h, Judy, he's – he's been asking for you. Dad keeps slipping in and out. Oh, God, he's so p-pale."

With each sob Mother's body shook violently.

I said, "Mother, I want to see Dad. Where is he?"

Before she could answer, Randy broke in, "Sis, they won't let anyone in but Mom. And then it's only for a few moments. You might as well just take a load off your feet and sit down." His voice trailed off as he added, "I'm afraid it's going to be a long haul."

Well, once I set my mind to something I don't let the word "no" stand in my way. Finding out my father's whereabouts, I located some surgical clothing and headed for his bedside.

When I first saw Dad, I felt as if someone had slammed his fist into my midriff. It took every ounce of my strength to walk over to his bed. Placing my hand on his, I began to speak in a wavering voice, "Dad... Dad... it's me, Judy. I'm here, hon. Come on..."

48

My throat began to tighten but I went on, "You can make it. After all, we've got that fishing trip to go on." Swallowing, I rushed to finish my thought. "We've got to see who catches the big one," I said quickly.

At that moment I swear I saw my father's eyelids flutter. In the next instant one of the doctors came up behind me, laid his hand on my shoulder and said, "Harold can't hear you. You'd best leave now. You're not sup-"

The doctor's voice broke off abruptly as Dad's heart monitor began to beep wildly and the needle gyrated erratically. Right then I knew the doctor was wrong. Dad did hear me!

As they began to work on him, someone hustled me out of the room. With a little bit more hope than when I first went into Dad's room, I rejoined Mother and my brothers.

Travis lifted his head and Randy pulled himself out of his chair. Mother leaned forward on the couch. All of them hoped eagerly for some news of improvement. "Any change?" Randy asked. "Did he come to?"

I shook my head. "I know he heard me, though," I said, "because just before they rushed me out, his eyelids moved and his heart monitor reacted strangely."

Three days and nights passed as we waited. Finally, on the fourth day, at 5 AM, a doctor came in and he broke our strained silence to announce, "We have moved Mr. Vail out of the Intensive Care Unit. His condition has stabilized and even improved somewhat." As relief flooded our faces, he smiled kindly and continued, "You may see him but only one at a time and only for five minutes each. You will find Harold in room 408." We thanked him and headed for the elevator.

After much persuasion Mother and I gained the doctor's consent to sit with Dad. We took turns of six-on and six-off shifts. Our spirits rose as we watched Dad improve. The doctors admitted he was making remarkable progress but they cautioned us not to expect too much.

When Dad was in his second week of therapy and all seemed to be going well, I began to make plans to return to Colorado. Thank God, I thought, this time my premonition had gone amiss.

On the night of the day before I was to leave, however, I awoke with the sensation that someone was standing over me. And there at the end of my bed stood my father. His feet did not seem to be touching the floor.

49

He spoke in a low, sad voice. "Judy girl, I'm going to die soon, and I must warn you that there will be those who will cause great difficulty and hardship for Mom."

I interrupted, "No – no – you're not going to die. You're not dead!"

Realizing that my voice was rising and not wanting to frighten Mother who slept just down the hall, I stopped.

Dad went on, "You must listen. I don't have much time, so hear me good. Mom is going to need your help with financial papers and to be protected from the one who plans to take advantage of her and of my death. You must not let this happen. Protect. Watch…" Before he and his voice faded, I heard him say, "I love you, Judy girl. Take care of Mom for me."

I lay there trying to decide if I should awaken Mother and tell her what had happened. Finally, I rose and went to her room.

It was unnecessary to wake her. In the dimly lit room I could see her lying there with her eyes wide open. My mouth felt dry as I told her, "Mother, I have something to tell you. I don't know if you will believe me but… I think you should know." My legs threatened to buckle and I sat down on the edge of her bed. Then I told her of my communication from Dad. She listened quietly. Once I had finished, she patted my hand and in a husky whisper said, "I believe you, dear."

There was a long silence between us. Then I said, "Mom, I think I ought to cancel my plans and not go back to Colorado."

"No," my mother said with conviction. "You go ahead and return like you planned, Judy. We mustn't intervene in God's will."

Knowing there was nothing further to say, I returned to my room.

At 10 o'clock that morning, against my better judgment, I pulled out of Mother's driveway on my way home. A week later, on November 19, I awoke in the early hours of the morning feeling cold. Even under the heavy blankets and with the room at 75 degrees, I knew Father had died. Later that morning a phone call confirmed my conviction. Once again, with a heavy heart I prepared to leave for Iowa City.

We buried Father on November 21, 1975, and his warning to me to expect trouble began to be fulfilled the next day. All he had predicted came true.

Perhaps it was reasonable of Dad to expect difficulties. At the time Dad died he and Mother were not legally married. Mother and Dad had been divorced nine years before and then the family had been united due to a double crisis. Mother was involved in a serious automobile accident which nearly took her life and her father – our grandfather – had a serious heart attack. In silence and without apologies we had all come together.

FATE February 1986

# NORMAN VINCENT PEALE'S PSYCHIC VISION
## Martin Ebon

I was returning from a European conference of the Parapsychology Foundation, traveling on one of the great transatlantic liners, probably the *Queen Mary,* when I was invited to have dinner at the captain's table. I felt very honored by this distinction. And, fitting the category of author, I found myself sitting next to one of the most popular inspirational writers of the day, the Reverend Norman Vincent Peale, whose book *The Power of Positive Thinking* has had a lasting impact for decades now.

The seating at the captain's table had clearly been hurried and rather haphazard, and no one really knew who anyone else was. But I did recognize the kindly, bespectacled gentleman to my right. And he, obviously trying to put a young man at ease, asked me cordially what I had chosen from the menu. Feeling just a bit wicked, I grinned at him sideways and said, "I am trying to think positively about the poached salmon!" At this he laughed heartily, and the conversational ice was broken.

Once Peale discovered where I had just come from, that I was the administrative secretary of the Parapsychology Foundation, working under its president, the well-known medium Eileen I. Garrett, he was full of questions. Frankly, I never had a chance to ask him anything. He was particularly interested in Mrs. Garrett's work with Dr. J.B. Rhine, director of the Parapsychology Laboratory, then affiliated with Duke University. Dr. Rhine was really something of a godfather for modern parapsychological research.

Peale had read Rhine's books and was keen to know more about the man's life and personality. Because I had accompanied Eileen Garrett several times on her visits to Dr. Rhine's laboratory in Durham, North Carolina, I was able to convey something about his tough, no-nonsense personality, his early theology studies, and his outdoorsman's habit of chopping wood and stomping around the wooded North Carolina countryside.

Peale seemed a bit disappointed when I mentioned that Rhine had really abandoned his direct studies in life after death as a result of experiments he undertook with Eileen Garrett. Simply put, what had happened was that Mrs. Garrett achieved the same results in Rhine's extrasensory perception (ESP) tests whether she was in a trance and the answers were given by apparent discarnate entities, or whether she was responding to the tests as herself. Rhine felt that this suggested that Garrett's personal ESP was at work, rather than the apparent insight of her seeming spirit controls, of whom the best known went by the name Abdul Latif.

What I did not realize at the time, and what only Peale's later statements and writings indicated, was that he also was deeply concerned with the subject of human personality survival after death. Of course, as an active Christian minister, the concept of immortality was integral to the faith he preached. But he was clearly involved in anything that might provide scientific proof of humanity's eternal life. What I did not know was that Peale himself had experienced several encounters with startling manifestations that suggested the survival of his own loved ones.

Dr. Peale died at age 95, on December 24, 1993, at his estate in Pawling, New York. Ruth (she is the former Loretta Ruth Stafford), his wife of 63 years, was by his bedside. *The New York Times* spoke of him as "one of the most influential religious figures of his time." The paper added that he "helped create a spiritual tone in the postwar United States with sermons, broadcasts, newspaper columns and books." It noted that Peale "told presidents and business executives and millions of other people that a proper state of mind, induced by simple prayer, could produce spiritual and material success on earth."

*Norman Vincent Peale.*

Looking back, I can see a certain kinship between Norman Vincent Peale and Joseph Banks Rhine. Both men were controversial, maintaining embattled positions, and, on occasion, could not but feel defensive. A critical biography, *God's Salesman,* by Carol V.R. George, recalled that "Peale studied the literature of psychic research and was familiar with J.B. Rhine's experiments at Duke University." Martin Gardner, the researcher critic of the paranormal, noted in an article on "Pealeism and the Paranormal" (*The Skeptical Inquirer,* Winter 1994) that Peale's "central themes" were reminiscent of "New Thought," a "religious movement that flourished in the decades before and after 1900," with roots in the transcendentalism of [Ralph Waldo] Emerson and sparked by the teachings of a Maine faith healer named Phineas Quimby."

The George biography recalls that, "with neither embarrassment nor hesitation," Peale revealed "his personal experiences with psychic phenomena" in sermons and speeches. These experiences were mainly "encounters with intimates who had died." Dr. Peale specifically dealt with the topic "Why I Believe in Life After Death" in the magazine *Guideposts* (April 1977), published by his Foundation for Christian Living.

He described having lunch with a "well-known British publisher" in London (Lord Thompson, who owned *The Times* and *Sunday Times* of London and *The Scotsman* of Edinburgh). Near the end of the meal, the publisher "turned to me suddenly and asked point-blank, 'Doctor Peale, do you really believe in life after death?' "

Peale answered, "Yes, I really do. I believe, because the Bible tells us that God's creation man is a spiritual being and things of the spirit are eternal."

Lord Thompson replied: "I want to believe that, but intellectually I find it difficult. I wish we had time to discuss it further."

Peale went on to describe that people, often in the prime of life, came to tell him that they were "haunted by a fear of death that they try to conceal from other people, and even from themselves." He added that he admitted to such people that "I, too, have moments when I flinch from the thought of dying."

Peale's father, who died at age 85 after a distinguished career as both a physician and minister, had "struggled against a very real fear of death." But, "not long after he died, my stepmother dreamed that he came to her and told her that his fears had been groundless." He said to her, "Don't ever worry about dying. There's nothing to it." She woke up astounded, and Peale felt that "my father did come to reassure her, because that is precisely the phrase I had heard him use a thousand times to dismiss something as unimportant or trivial."

Peale had a similar experience after his mother died, in 1939. He wrote: "I was alone in my office, numb with grief and loss. There was a Bible on my desk, and I put my hand on it, staring blindly out the window. As I did so, I felt a pair of hands touch my head, gently, lovingly, unmistakably. The pressure lasted only an instant; then it was gone again. An illusion? A hallucination caused by grief? I don't think so. I think my mother was permitted to reach across the gulf of death to touch and reassure me."

Dr. Peale also recalled the appearance of an apparition of his father. This occurred as he was attending a Methodist meeting at Sea Island, Georgia. The meeting, conducted by Bishop Arthur J. Moore, was attended by several thousand participants. When Bishop Moore asked the clergy among the huge congregation to come to the front of the hall, several hundred started walking down the aisles. As Peale looked at the throng, he saw his father marching among them. Peale, looking down from the speakers' platform, remembered the scene this way:

"And suddenly, among them, I saw my father. I saw him as plainly as I ever saw him when he was alive. He seemed about 40, vital and handsome. He was singing with the others. When he smiled at me and put up his hand in an old familiar gesture, for several unforgettable seconds it was as if my father and I were alone in that big auditorium. Then he was gone, but in my heart the certainty of his presence was indisputable. He was there, and I know that someday, somewhere, I'll meet him again."

Yet another after-death encounter involved Peale's brother Robert, who had been a physician. The two men were emotionally close. In 1970, shortly after Bob's death, Norman Vincent Peale was speaking to a group of members of his foundation at Pawling, New York. Suddenly, although separated by two walls, he saw his brother walking outside the building.

It so happened that after Peale became a minister, his brother had taken to calling him "Deacon." And, on this occasion, the seeming apparition waved to him and said, "It's okay, Deacon. It's okay." Again, as in the case of his father's ghostly manifestation, Peale's brother appeared younger than he had been at the time of his death; he seemed quite youthful, in his 40s.

As people who have had psychic experience often observe, the meaning of such encounters may be quite unremarkable; or, at least, not terribly dramatic or significant. This was the case with an assurance Peale received from his deceased mother in the late 1940s. He had attended an auction at Asbury Park, New Jersey, where he bought two fancy hurricane lamps as a surprise gift for his wife, Ruth. He paid $400 for them and was wondering whether she might not take him to task for having been extravagant and overpaid for the lamps.

Peale, in his best folksy manner, recalled later that on the highway from New Jersey to New York, he stopped at a Howard Johnson's restaurant for a hot dog. In this everyday setting, he heard his mother's voice telling him, "Don't worry about it. Ruth is a wonderful girl. Anything you get for her, she deserves." Despite the relatively trivial occasion and the undramatic environment, Peale was so deeply touched by this encounter that he wept.

Now, let us keep in mind that Norman Vincent Peale communicated these intimate personal experiences, over and over, to a wide public. Despite his great popularity as a peace of mind preacher, telling about such psychic encounters involved the risk of being ridiculed or viewed as someone given to over-emotional, even pathological, visual and auditory hallucinations. I am well aware that such ghostly encounters are viewed by some deeply believing Christians as contacts with demons – others, perhaps more given to positive thinking, may regard them as encounters with angels. To Peale, these were significant personal experiences that helped to round out his views of life, death, faith and daily living.

His own encounters made him understanding and supportive of the experiences of others. When author Susy Smith published her book, *Confessions of a Psychic,* which vividly described both the challenges and high risks of mediumship, Peale commented that this "courageous" work proved her to be "a sensitive person of a high order, gifted with profound qualities of insight" and "a master of intuitive truth."

I can well understand why he had been more interested in Dr. J.B. Rhine's accounts of individual spontaneous psychic encounters than by Rhine's much less dramatic laboratory experiments. In his book, *The Amazing Results of Positive Thinking,* Peale devoted a chapter to Rhine's research, but ignored his statistical testing altogether. This difficult, repetitive, quantitative work preceded today's intricate computer-aided parapsychology studies.

What kind of cases interested Peale? He started off by citing the experience of a middle-aged man who was driving his car along a New Jersey highway and suddenly felt a terrible pain in his chest. The pain was so severe that he stopped his car, thinking he was having a heart attack, although he soon recovered. But, "a few hours later, he learns that his son, driving in Colorado, had been killed at that exact moment, his chest crushed by the wheel of his car." Peale asked, "And this mystic force?"

"Telepathy."

Well, yes. And more. precisely, crisis telepathy, perhaps the most dramatic of all reported psychic experiences.

Yet researchers know that this kind of experience is exceedingly difficult to substantiate. Efforts to track down and carefully document this type of spontaneous phenomena depend on the testimony of reliable witnesses, people who remember events, times and places with the kind of accuracy that proves maddeningly elusive.

Peale told his readers that he regarded such experiences as "evidence of greater capacity within yourself, a capacity that can aid you in living a stronger, more effective life."

Peale also quoted a letter he had received from a professor at a New England college, a man who told the story of how he had been bothered in the past by debilitating headaches. These, the professor related, "were always relieved when my grandmother, who made her home with my parents, would place her hand on my forehead."

Later, during his first year of teaching at Amherst College, Massachusetts, he had such a severe headache that he went to bed early. That night, "Toward midnight, I suddenly felt my grandmother standing beside my bed. She placed her hand on my head and the pain ceased, never to return." He heard later that his grandmother "had passed on at the very hour when I felt her hand on my head. I am sure that she thus took the first opportunity to bring me the relief she alone could give."

J.B. Rhine used to feel that throughout his career he had to fight a two-front battle: on the one hand, he had to deal with the never-to-be-satisfied skeptics; on the other hand, he had to fend off the all-believing occultists. As *The New York Times* noted, Norman Vincent Peale was accused of "simplifying Christianity by avoiding deeper confrontations with sin and guilt." But he also was castigated as advocating an intrusive religiosity that clashed with the tolerances of a secular society.

Writing came naturally to Peale. Born on May 31, 1898, in Bowersville, Ohio, he graduated from Ohio Wesleyan University in 1920 and started as a reporter on the *Detroit Journal*. As he recalled later, he felt a sudden call to the ministry after he talked a frightened child off a ledge during an apartment fire.

His first pastorate was in Rhode Island. Then, in 1924, he moved and became pastor at the Kings Highway Church in Brooklyn, New York. During the three years he served there, the congregation grew from 40 to

1,000. In 1930, while working toward his doctorate, he married Loretta Ruth Stafford, who was also a student at Syracuse University.

The central period of Peale's career, from 1932 to 1984, was spent at Marble Collegiate Church on New York City's Fifth Avenue. When he became pastor, during the Depression, the church only had a congregation of 600.

By the time he retired in 1984, membership had reached 5,000, and additional audiences listened over closed-circuit television in adjoining rooms.

While Peale was essentially pragmatic, asking his public to utilize his findings and insights toward a happier and more successful life, he was undogmatic about the application of potential psychic abilities. He concluded, "But even if the day of our practical use of such phenomena should be far off, we cannot avoid the belief that man will become ultimately master of forces in the psychic realm, as he is in the material."

*Martin Ebon (1917-2006): Prolific author on parapsychology topics.*

FATE December 1994

# MEDIUMSHIP

# MAKING CONTACT: DO WE LIVE AFTER WE DIE?
## Alan Vaughan

Can the dead contact the living? This age-old question is increasingly finding a positive answer. In a poll conducted by Andrew Greeley of the National Opinion Research Council, 44 per cent of American adults reported that they had been in contact with the dead. Among a group of widows interviewed, an amazing 67 per cent said that their deceased husbands had been in touch with them. Such a high incidence of spontaneous mediumship suggests that channeling ability must be a widespread, normal human ability. Yet the science establishment seems to interpret such findings as indicative of the human ability to hallucinate – or at least the tendency for people to fool themselves. What evidence do we have that might convince modern doubting Thomases?

### Spontaneous materialization
The history of Spiritualism is filled with reports of materializations in dark seance rooms – and many accusations of fraud. Does bodily

materialization ever happen in broad daylight and to people who are not mediums? Among the many stories I have heard, two stand out:

In an interview with a Chicago newspaper, death researcher Elizabeth Kübler-Ross described a materialization she witnessed. One day when she was despairing at losing so many clients to death and thinking about leaving the field, Kübler-Ross looked up from her desk and was astonished to see standing there a woman client who had died some months previously. The materialized woman urged her to continue her important work. Trying to convince herself that she was not hallucinating, Kübler-Ross asked the entity to sign a piece of paper. The woman did, and then vanished with a smile. Kübler-Ross hurried to her cabinet and located that patient's file. The signature matched. The experience inspired Kübler-Ross to continue with her work.

While living in Czechoslovakia some years ago, author Bernard Hutton was writing a book on the famous Czech composer, Friedrich Smetana, (1824-1884), whose *Ma Vlast* endures today. Hutton was having difficulty with a chapter on an important period of Smetana's life because there were no records of it to be found. Seated at his typewriter, Hutton fumed in frustration and wondered how he would ever find material on the missing years.

Suddenly the dead composer appeared in Hutton's office. Hutton recognized him from a portrait. The spectral composer appeared to be solid and lifelike. Smetana spoke to Hutton in archaic Czech and explained what had happened during the missing years. Startled, Hutton turned on his tape recorder. Smetana said that the missing records could be found in a small museum in a suburb of Prague. Smetana then vanished as mysteriously as he had come.

A bewildered Hutton played the tape to convince himself that he was not hallucinating. The archaic Czech was recorded exactly as he had heard it. Hutton journeyed to the museum and he found the missing records. He was now able to complete his book, which was a success – thanks to an encore appearance by Smetana.

Can human consciousness persist for thousands of years after death? Could that consciousness communicate in a meaningful way? Could that ancient voice speak in a tongue long dead?

Those questions came to mind when I began to channel 20 years ago. As a science textbook editor in New York, I was skeptical of such claims.

Not a paragraph, not a line of my science books suggested that human consciousness survived death, let alone spoke from beyond the grave.

## Speaking dead languages

One evening during a discussion with an artist friend, Jim, he mentioned that his roommate – I will call her Helen – was trance channeling an entity that lived 2,000 years ago in the eastern Mediterranean. Helen would go into trance, watch letters of the alphabet appear one by one, and call them out to Jim, who transcribed the messages. Remarkably, the messages were in a dead foreign language – Koine Greek, as they finally learned from the entity. Helen was a talented theater producer and has since won many awards, but neither she nor Jim had any knowledge of ancient Greek. They finally located a translator who put the messages into English. Jim gave me a copy of the transcripts.

A few phrases had eluded the translator. One was "pan opeac." The translator suggested that "pan" could mean "all." But "opeac" did not seem like Greek at all. I wondered if perhaps a mistake had been made in the transliteration from the Greek alphabet to the Roman. Perhaps "p" should be "r" and "c" should be "s." That would make it "oreas," but I had never heard that word either. I checked my Greek dictionary and discovered that it was a rare epithet of the god Pan and referred to the mountain Oreas. So, the god Pan came into the case, making it even more mysterious.

Another word that the translator could not initially find meant "pineal gland." The startling aspect of that word was that it came in response to the question of how it was possible for the entity to communicate through Helen.

Can human consciousness persist for thousands of years after death? Could the pineal gland plays an important role in psychic channeling. Even more important as a scientific criterion, Helen was displaying responsive xenoglossy – answering questions in an unstudied foreign language.

When I explained my findings to Jim, he was intrigued by the pineal gland information, but he was absolutely astonished at the reference to Pan. "During the period when Helen was getting those messages," explained Jim, "I had a compulsion to try a new kind of artwork. I call it sand painting. I made three-dimensional reliefs of sand molded like rock. The first sand painting was of the great god Pan."

The entity also supplied pages of elegant poetry written in classical Greek. The poems described a festival of lights and a procession taking place at Eleusis, the site of a mystery cult that worshiped Demeter and Dionysius. This influential cult persisted for thousands of years, but no one knew the details of what went on. Cult members were forbidden to reveal its secrets on pain of death. Consequently, there is no published source to which the channeled poetry could be compared. By the same token, Helen could not have acquired this information in any normal way.

A dead language also plays a role in a remarkable project being undertaken by the Research Center for Applied Intuition in Redwood City, California. Here, sounds of ancient Egyptian speech are being entered into a computer. Dr. William Kautz, director of the project, is producing a dictionary of ancient Egyptian as spoken 3,000 years ago.

The remarkable aspect of this project is that the ancient Egyptian source material came through a British medium during the 1930s. Two researchers, Dr. E H. Wood and Howard Hulme, recorded the utterances of "Lady Nona," who claimed to be a past-life personality of the medium, Rosemary, and a consort of Pharaoh Amenhotep III. The transcripts contain more than 5,000 phrases, and the researchers also obtained a sound recording.

Egyptologists have had mixed reactions to this purported psychic solution to the puzzle of how ancient Egyptian was spoken. Most of the vocalizations these experts have proposed for ancient Egyptian speech are guesswork.

Kautz predicts that "detailed knowledge of this speech, long sought unsuccessfully by Egyptologists, would provide important clues to understanding the form of communication used in this greatest of ancient cultures."

Another possible confirmation of the voice from ancient Egypt comes from a prediction made by Lady Nona that a scroll validating her story will be found in a tomb soon to be discovered in Upper Egypt.

The prevailing view among parapsychologists, echoing the late J. B. Rhine's sentiments, is that if you could prove that what a medium says about a dead person is true – either by testimony from persons who knew the deceased or by documents – then you could also explain it away as due to ESP.

Here is a case that defies even that catch-22: On October 5, 1930, Britain was horrified at the news that their ultimate wonder of the sky, the dirigible R-101, had exploded over France on its maiden voyage. Two days later, during an experiment at the National Laboratory of Psychical Research in London, researcher Harry Price had medium Eileen Garrett in trance. A male voice apologized for interfering. He gave his name as Flight Commander H. Carmichael Irwin, captain of the R-101. The Irwin personality spoke through Mrs. Garrett, giving a detailed description of the engineering faults that led to the crash of the R-101. No living person could possibly have known those details; they were only discovered much later in an intensive investigation by the British Air Ministry. An aviation expert compared the Garrett transcript with the Ministry's published report. Every single detail was confirmed. Most persuasive of all was the motive expressed by Irwin – to try to prevent future air disasters.

Here are some excerpts from Irwin's communication. (Bracketed comments are from an aviation expert, based on the Air Ministry's report.)

"Explosion caused by friction in electric storm. Flying too low altitude and could never rise. [Very probable; borne out by evidence at inquiry.] Disposable lift could not be utilized. Load too great for long flight. Same with SL-8. Tell Eckener. [SL-8 has been verified as the number of a German airship, SL standing for Schutte Lanz. This was verified only after going through complete records of German airships. Dr. Eckener is the constructor of the Graf Zeppelin. ...

"Engines wrong – too heavy – cannot rise. [In accordance with known facts.] Never reached cruising altitude – same on trials. Too short trials. [Yes, admittedly.] No one knew the ship properly.

"Airscrews too small. [Believed by many informed opinions to be correct.] Fuel injection bad and air pump failed. Cooling system bad. Bore capacity bad... 1100 c.c. but that bore is not enough to raise too heavy load and support weight. It has been known to me on many occasions that the bore capacity was entirely inadequate to the volume of structure. [Language technically correct and might have been Irwin's opinion. It is an opinion that would only be expressed by an expert.] ...

"Fabric all water-logged and ship's nose is down. [True.] Impossible to rise. [Right.] ... new type of feed absolutely and entirely wrong. [The feed had been changed from a motor feed to a handpump feed.] Two hours tried to rise but elevator jammed ...

"At inquiry to be held later it will be found that the superstructure of the envelope contained no resilience and had far too much weight in envelope. [Correct.] This was not so until March of this year when no security was made by adding of super-steel structure. I knew then that this was not a dream but a nightmare... From beginning of trouble, I knew we had not a chance, knew it to be the feed, and we could never rise... "

Some of the details channeled to Garrett were known to no living person. The evidence strongly points to Irwin as the only possible source of the information. A 1988 *Time-Life* book on psychic powers disputes this evidence, saying that all the information could have come from someone present at the seance. Yet that obviously could not be true. Detailed news of the crash had not yet reached England when the seance was held. Confirmation of many statements was still in the future – to be discovered by the Air Ministry's inquiry.

Eileen Garrett's considerable talent as a medium – communicating highly technical information beyond her own knowledge – enabled the R-101 case to provide the highest quality of evidence for· survival of consciousness beyond death. The ESP catch-22 should finally be put to rest.

## The meaning of mediumship

British psychical researcher Alan Gauld has extensively reviewed the investigations of traditional mediumship in *The Handbook of Parapsychology*. His chapter on "Discarnate Survival" lists 242 major books and journal reports giving scientific evidence of survival. The moot question was always, "Can spirits, if they exist, communicate through mediums?"

We cannot rely on secondhand experiences of professional mediums. We ourselves have to attempt to make contact with discarnate consciousness. If several of us pick up similar information about a target discarnate person, then we can form a consensus of experience. In other words, communicating with discarnate entities would become part of our consensual reality. We would not have to take anyone's word for it; we would experience it ourselves.

Once you open the door to higher consciousness, you take a step that forever changes who you are.

*Alan Vaughan (1936-2001): Psychic, author and researcher of parapsychology topics. This article is adapted from a chapter in Vaughan's book,* Doorways to Higher Consciousness.

FATE June 1995

# PSYCHIC GEORGE ANDERSON SPOKE TO OUR MURDERED SON
## Alfred Anzalone

On the night after my son was buried, a violent thunderstorm struck. Bolts of lightning blazed across the sky, bathing the majestic clouds in brilliant white bursts of pure energy. I knew then that John had crossed over and was being welcomed into heaven.

"It was God's will."

"He's in a better place now."

A child's death is the ultimate torment, and people should be aware that they cannot lessen grieving parents' pain by making these statements. Yet, their mere utterance implies that something, someplace, does exist after we die. Since my son's brutal murder five years ago, I have become fascinated with the concept of a spiritual world. The comforting belief that John's spirit resides in a place other than memory has enabled my wife and me to cope with our grief.

Like thunderstorms, grief is an awesome force, a downpour that drowns the survivors of a child's death in total desolation. Denial and depression are the consequences of this psychological storm. Losing a child is too painful, and many parents are unable to cope with their loss. Parents who must endure this torture want to hold onto the memory and spirit of their child and should not be discouraged from seeking support and help from religious faith, family, friends – and George Anderson.

Almost a year after John's tragic death in June 1990, my wife and I were urged by a friend to relieve our sorrow with a psychic reading. Our search led us to George Anderson, a psychic medium who is able to receive and discern spiritual messages. In their informative book *Our Children Forever: George Anderson's Messages from Children on the Other Side,* Joel Martin and Patricia Romanowski clearly emphasize that Anderson's clairvoyance takes place in a fully conscious state and with no knowledge about the bereaved people who seek out his talent. The authors point out that he sees faces, events, letters and numbers in his mind's eye, enabling him to feel and know the facts about a loved one's life – and death. George Anderson's psychometry is a neutral, passive conduit between the physical and the spiritual worlds.

The theory of life after death is based on numerous case histories in which people have "died" but later revived. These histories have several elements in common:

> 1) The float: An out-of-body sensation of floating upward while observing one's body from a detached level.
> 2) The tunnel: A void that the spirit travels through at incredible speed.
> 3) The light: An all-encompassing serenity welcoming the spirit to a place of unbelievable beauty and grace.
> 4) The meeting: A reunion with loved ones who have passed on before and who now welcome the spirit into the otherworld.

These four basic phenomena best describe what George Anderson terms crossover. Crossover is the death of the body and the birth of the spirit into a world of immense peace – and love.

To appreciate the full impact of my tape-recorded psychometric reading with Anderson, I must briefly highlight the facts of my son's life and his untimely death.

Some people live 60 or 70 years and never touch anyone, but John lived only 21 years and touched everyone he met. From childhood, he always had a timidity, a shyness, that lingered with him into young adulthood. He lacked aggressiveness and saw only the good in people. He placed his trust in human nature. It was his naivete that ultimately led to his death.

John had met, fallen in love with and married Andrea, a foxy, impetuous girl who completely intoxicated him. During this time, Andrea's sister, Gina, was dating Jason, a quiet, enigmatic, older man whom John befriended and asked to be in his wedding party.

Shortly after John and Andrea married, Gina ended her relationship with Jason. Unable to cope with their breakup, Jason lured John to a deserted warehouse in Brooklyn, New York, and pleaded with him to intercede on his behalf to win Gina back. When John did not promise to help, Jason shot him in the chest, placed his body in the trunk of Jason's car, and drove to Maine, where he feebly attempted suicide in a motel. My son died at the hands of a coward who could not handle basic human emotions. John was the victim of a love gone wrong for which he had no responsibility and no influence.

## The reading

It was a warm August day in 1991 when my wife, Joanne, and I arrived at George Anderson's home. I was not sure what to expect. There were no tents, no crystal balls, no walls painted black with sparkling stars, and no Tarot cards. It was simply a modest house nestled in a quiet, suburban community in Deer Park, New York. An assistant led us into a living room furnished with more than a dozen chairs and a sofa. Other people were in the room, all burdened by the loss of a loved one.

George Anderson walked in. His presence bathed the room with a priestly grace. Already, my apprehension fizzled down to a calm curiosity. Anderson's pepper and salt beard surrounded a warm, dimpled smile, and his dark, intense eyes scanned each face as he softly spoke. He announced to the group that although we were there to seek comfort from a departed loved one, he might receive messages from other spirits and therefore we must not be disappointed. He also advised that certain attitudes and feelings of those who have passed on transfer into the otherworld. After crossing over, the loved one will enter a more serene state free of hate, fear and pain.

Scribbling on a pad, Anderson randomly approached each member of the group. I soon realized this writing was a form of concentration, a psychic doodling of initials, names and symbols.

He cautioned us to respond with a simple yes or no unless more specific interpretation of a name was required.

I watched and listened as Anderson spoke to each of the bereaved. A chill ran through my body when they responded in tears and joy upon hearing messages of love and faith from beyond this world. Joanne and I stiffened when he approached us, his pencil busily scratching on the pad. I pressed the record button on my tape recorder.

"A young male has crossed over recently?" he asked.

"Yes," I responded.

"Is there a Frank?" (Frank was my father-in-law who died four years earlier and to whom John was very close.) "Frank is speaking in Italian." (Frank spoke broken English but preferred to use Italian.) "I am also getting a Bill or William." (William was my father, who died 13 years before.) "They are there with the young man and helped him to cross over. I am getting the name of John. Is this your son?"

"Yes," my wife sobbed.

"Your son passed tragically. His death was beyond his control. He keeps saying he is sorry about what happened, and there was nothing he could do about it." Anderson paused and scratched on the pad. "Did your son have a problem with his health? I keep getting a breathing difficulty, something to do with his chest." Another pause. "I get a piercing of his chest, something going into his heart. Your son was victimized. He was stabbed or shot, hence that piercing feeling. Your son was murdered, but not deliberately. He was stalked and shot at close range in his chest. His death occurred near a time of festivity, which may explain why he is carrying white roses for a special occasion."

We responded that John's murder occurred just before Memorial Day, shortly before our wedding anniversary. Anderson's pencil was busy again. My skepticism was rapidly fading. In a few short moments this stranger already knew my son's name, how he had died, and the names of both grandfathers who had loved him so much.

"Was your son involved in the wrong crowd?" he asked.

"No," we replied.

"He was with the wrong person. He was cornered, but it was not a crime like robbery, although I sense his murderer was emotionally robbed. He had a personal problem and argued with your son. They were alone, but out of the house." Anderson's eyes focused upon me. "The guy just went off the wall! He lost it. He became emotionally unhinged. John knew him, trusted him, called him a friend. Yet, he cornered John, accused him of taking something, but not money. John was shocked. His assailant had no particular reason to kill him. Your son trusted him and considered him a friend. His friend imagined the worst in people and was subject to schizoid outbursts. He shot your son in cold blood. Your son forgives him."

By this time, I was convinced that Anderson was actually in communication with John. His depiction of John's killer was uncanny. Coincidence? Perhaps. Anyone who murders can be considered emotionally unhinged. Lucky guess? I don't think so. The murder trial had revealed how Jason was subject to schizoid outbursts.

"Pray for his spirit... "

Anderson kept moving the pencil. "Your son asks that you pray for his spirit to the Blessed Mother. He says that someone has been saying the Rosary for him. It is a powerful form of prayer."

My wife confirmed that her mother says the Rosary.

"You yourself cannot pray and are having trouble with prayer," Anderson said to Joanne.

"I have difficulty, yes," she replied.

"John is asking that you pray to the Blessed Mother and to be spiritual. He sends you his love." Anderson's warm, comforting smile soothed us. "Your son was kind of naive, kind of an innocent young man with very little street smarts. He basically looked for the good in people and was forgiving of their faults. He is sorry and apologetic, but he cannot help it, as that was the kind of guy he was. There is no place for hate in the otherworld. He thanks you for any prayers you could offer."

The pencil kept scarring the pad. It was as if John were guiding Anderson's hand. "Is there a Peter or Pete?"

"Yes. Peter is his older brother," I replied. (That's it. I believe!)

"He is calling for Peter. Obviously, they were very close. Again, he is asking that you forgive him for what has happened. John keeps

75

calling to his brother, Peter. I am also getting the name of a close female, but the name seems to be that of an Andrew or Andy."

"She was John's wife, Andrea. They were married for only six months," I answered. A voice in my mind kept tugging at me: "But how does he know?"

"Yes, of course, Andy could be a nickname for Andrea." He paused. "The murder happened in Brooklyn or Queens?"

"Yes, it occurred in a warehouse near the Brooklyn-Queens border," I said. The only way he could have known where the murder took place was if John had told him.

"John and his friend went out together, then there were gunshots, with no apparent motive. John reassures you that he is at peace and no harm can ever come to him again. Do you plan on moving?"

"No," Joanne replied.

"John says you will be moving soon." (Approximately two years later, my wife and I moved to New Jersey to live closer to Peter, who has since been married.)

"John did not have any children?"

"No. He was married for only six months and wanted to save some money before having children," I said, realizing my answer was too explanatory and Anderson probably knew the answer, anyway.

"Again, he calls out that he is all right and has adjusted to his new world. And he is sorry for what happened."

## Messages of love

When the pencil stopped, I knew the reading was completed. Anderson advised that our grief was still strong and would be reinforced at times of celebration and anniversaries. He encouraged us to find strength in faith and to move on. At no point did Anderson attempt to sensationalize his ability. His voice was a bridge across the unseen waters of death from which messages of love, hope, faith and courage emerged. In my opinion, Anderson walks across uncharted waters. There was no reference point where he could ever have known the facts before our meeting. I felt as if I was in the presence of my beloved son and that he is truly safe with those loved ones who have crossed over before him.

Now, when a thunderstorm nears, I welcome its power, its energy, its light. Like death itself, after the storm has passed, I feel my spirit has crossed over into a renewed freshness and the world is a little more bearable.

FATE January 1996

# HOUDINI'S MESSAGE FROM BEYOND THE GRAVE
## Lydia Emery

When Harry Houdini died in 1926, he left behind a reputation of being probably the greatest stage magician who ever lived. He also left a record of exposing dozens of fraudulent spiritualistic mediums.

And, as his last effort in psychic investigation, he left a pact with his wife Beatrice by which he would communicate with her in secret code from beyond the grave – if he could.

So many attempts by mediums to show that Houdini had communicated were proved false in the years after his death that the general public still believes that all attempts to communicate with the master magician proved failures. But the facts are quite otherwise.

Houdini did communicate. He used the secret code which he had arranged with his wife Beatrice.

The communication was verified by Beatrice Houdini herself. And she attested to it both by affidavits and by a personal letter to Walter Winchell which he published in his column. The medium was the Rev.

Arthur Ford, then pastor of First Spiritualist Church, Carnegie Hall, New York City. Ford first entered the case in 1928, two years after Houdini's death, when he announced that he had a message from Houdini's mother. The key word was "FORGIVE."

This the newspapers denied, and the *Brooklyn Eagle* reported that Beatrice Houdini herself had spoken of this message in an interview in March 1927. Other newspapers denounced Ford, who was a protege of Sir Arthur Conan Doyle himself. Ford refused to allow himself to be drawn into a controversy on this matter. He was deeply immersed in sorrow over the recent death of his son, who died from exposure after falling through the ice while skating.

Instead, in November 1928, Ford sat in trance and received a second message from Houdini through his spirit collaborator, "Fletcher." The experiment began in Ford's hotel room and the message took 10 weeks to assemble in its entirety. Only one word at a time came through during the earlier seances.

"The first word," Fletcher said, "is the one that is going to unlock the rest." The word was "ROSABELLE."

Two weeks later a second word, "NOW," was added. In December, the third word was given. It was "LOOK," and was described as being the sixth word in the code.

During the Christmas holidays, "Fletcher" asked that the word "NOW" be withdrawn as possibly incorrect. Two other words, "RIGHT" and "NOW" were also brought through and later discarded. By the end of the year, three other new words had been added. They were "ANSWER," "PRAY" and "TELL."

Several days after the beginning of the year 1929, the seventh seance was conducted. The guide discovered only two errors in the message. They were to transpose the third and fourth words, and the last words, of the 10 complete words in the sequence.

"Fletcher" continued: "He (Houdini) tells me that he has put the next five words, explaining these, in French." The control had not deciphered them and therefore gave the other words in advance.

On January 5, 1929, the eighth and final seance took place. The last word of the second Houdini message was given. It was "TELL." This was followed by a dictated message which was to be written in longhand and delivered to Beatrice Houdini from her husband. This is the message:

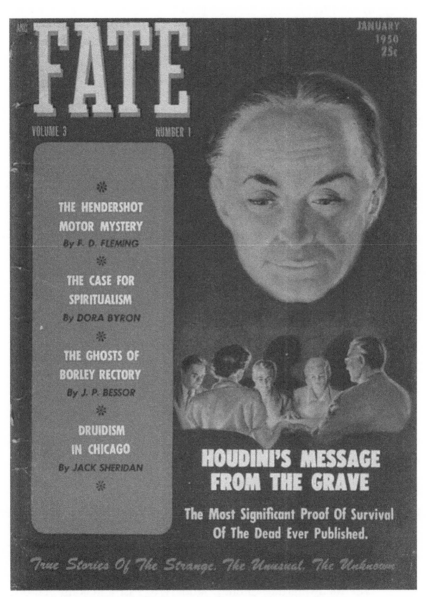

AND

# FATE

JANUARY
1950
25¢

VOLUME 3    NUMBER 1

❋

**THE HENDERSHOT MOTOR MYSTERY**
By F. D. FLEMING

❋

**THE CASE FOR SPIRITUALISM**
By DORA BYRON

❋

**THE GHOSTS OF BORLEY RECTORY**
By J. P. BESSOR

❋

**DRUIDISM IN CHICAGO**
By JACK SHERIDAN

❋

## HOUDINI'S MESSAGE FROM THE GRAVE

The Most Significant Proof Of Survival
Of The Dead Ever Published.

*True Stories Of The Strange, The Unusual, The Unknown*

*Cover of the 1950 FATE magazine featuring Houdini's afterlife code.*

"Harry Houdini, whose real name was Erich Weiss, is here and wishes to send to his wife, Beatrice Houdini, the 10-word code which he would do if it were possible to communicate. Houdini says you are to take this message to her, and upon acceptance of it, he wishes her to follow the plan they agreed upon prior to his passing."

Then the complete code message was repeated:

"ROSABELLE ANSWER TELL PRAY ANSWER LOOK TELL ANSWER ANSWER TELL!"

Upon completion of the note and the message, the letter was signed by those present at the Ford seance. They were Francis R. Fast, a New York broker and importer; Helen E. Morris; Dorothy Stafford; and John W. Stafford, associate editor of the *Scientific American*.

"Fletcher's" next speech was recorded stenographically by Fast and John Stafford:

"That last is the message which is to go to his (Houdini's) wife. He wants it signed in ink by each one present. He says the code is known only to him and his wife, and that no one on earth but those two know it. He says there is no danger on that score, and that she must make it public. It must come from her; you are nothing more than agents.

"He says ('Fletcher' continued) that when it comes through there will be a veritable storm, that many will seek to destroy her and she will be accused of everything that is not good, but she is honest enough to keep the pact which they repeated over and over before his death. The last words he spoke were those used in going over this together, so that they would understand it clearly. 'I know,' he says, 'that she will be happy, because neither of us believed that it would be possible.'

"Her husband says that on receipt of this message she must set a time, as soon as possible, when she will sit with this instrument Arthur Ford, while I, 'Fletcher,' speak to her, and after he has repeated this message to her, she is to return a code to him which will be understood by her and by him alone. The code that will be returned will be a supplement to this code, and the two together will spell a word which sums it all up, and that word will be the message that he wants to send back. He refuses to give that word until he gives it to her."

The following day, Sunday, January 6, Fast and John Stafford called at the Houdini home where Beatrice lived with her mother, Mrs. Balbonoa Rahner; her sister, Mrs. Marie Hinson, Mrs. Minnie Chester, and her life-long companion, Miss Julia Karchere.

Beatrice Houdini had been slightly injured in a fall on New Year's but nevertheless she received Fast and Stafford. They gave her the message.

Confronted with their testimony and with the code before her as proof, Mrs. Houdini agreed to a seance which was to be conducted at her home two days later on Tuesday, January 8. On that day, Ford, accompanied by three members of his group, and Harry R. Zander, a reporter of the United Press, called at Mrs. Houdini's home, 67 Payson Avenue. She lay on a couch and motioned her visitors to be seated.

Arthur Ford sat in a chair that had belonged to Houdini and fell into what appeared to be a deep slumber. The voice of "Fletcher" filled the room, speaking for Harry Houdini.

"Hello, Bess, sweetheart," came "Fletcher's" voice, then repeating the 10 words of the code.

"This code is one you used in one of your secret mind-reading acts," said "Fletcher's" voice. "Now Harry wants you to tell him whether they are right."

"Yes, they are," said Mrs. Houdini faintly.

"He smiles and says, 'Thank you,'" said "Fletcher" after a hesitation. There was another pause, then "Fletcher" said: "He now tells you to remove your wedding ring and to tell them what 'ROSABELLE' means."

Mrs. Houdini slipped the band from her left hand and sang:

*Rosabelle, sweet Rosabelle*
*I love you more than I can tell;*
*O'er me you cast a spell,*
*I love you! My Rosabelle!"*

As the song died on her lips the guide said, "He says, 'I thank you, darling. The first time I heard you sing that was years ago in our first show together.'"

The nine words succeeding "ROSABELLE" in the code message were to spell one word in the Houdini mind-reading code.

"Fletcher" explained the second word, which was "ANSWER," as representing the letter "B" – the second letter of the alphabet. The next word in the code was "TELL" and the fifth letter of the alphabet "E." The letter "L" being the 12th letter of the alphabet, the first and second words of the code were used to make up the 12 letters below:

ORIGINAL CODE
1. PRAY A
2. ANSWER B
3. SAY C
4. NOW D
5. TELL E
6. PLEASE F
7. SPEAK G
8. QUICKLY H
9. LOOK E
10. Be QUICK J

The first 10 letters of the alphabet were represented by 10 words, the 11th letter of the code beginning with one-one, followed by one-two, for the 12th, and so on until the alphabet was completed.

In order to receive the correct message, it was necessary that the correct sequence be followed, otherwise the letters would have been jumbled and another word supplanted.

At the conclusion of the seance, "Fletcher" gave forth the one key word that was made possible through the 10 separate words, several of them having been used in repetition. It was the single word "BELIEVE."

This is the deciphered code word sequence and its meaning:

| | |
|---|---|
| Answer | B |
| Tell | E |
| Prayer | L |
| Answer (1 & 2) | I |
| Look | E |
| Tell | V |
| Answer, Answer (2 & 2) Tell | E |

New York newspapers that evening were filled with news that Houdini's message had been delivered. John W. Stafford, the associate editor of *Scientific American,* said that he was "convinced, after attending several of the seances, that Harry Houdini, dead world-famous magician, talked through a medium with Mrs. Beatrice Houdini, his widow.

"In this case, accepting the good faith of all parties concerned, which I do, there can be no doubt that communication has been established between a living person and one dead," Stafford said.

While the newspapers were hailing the phenomenon, Mrs. Houdini, accompanied by those who had attended the seance at her home, rode to the Fifth Avenue branch of the Manufacturers' Trust Company and withdrew a sealed envelope that had been locked in the Houdini vault.

Before the witnesses, she broke the seal and laid the papers on a desk before them. The words were identical with those given by "Fletcher" while Arthur Ford was in a trance! Even the request that Mrs. Houdini remove her ring and sing "Rosabelle" had been set down as part of the test.

Following this, Beatrice Houdini worded a dated statement on her own stationery which declared the message given her by Arthur Ford to be correct in every detail. Her signature was witnessed by Harry R. Zander, the United Press representative; Mrs. Minnie Chester and John W. Stafford. This is the wording of the statement:

New York City
January 9th, 1929


REGARDLESS OF ANY STATEMENTS MADE TO THE CONTRARY, I WISH TO DECLARE THAT THE MESSAGE IN ITS ENTIRETY, AND IN THE AGREED UPON SEQUENCE, GIVEN TO ME BY ARTHUR FORD, IS THE CORRECT MESSAGE PREARRANGED BETWEEN MR. HOUDINI AND MYSELF.


Beatrice Houdini
WITNESSED:
Harry R. Zander
Minnie Chester
John W. Stafford


85

Mrs. Houdini later told reporters who interviewed her that it would have been impossible for her mind to have been read. She said: "I never saw Mr. Ford or any of the persons with him until that day. Of course, I knew that code, but I had no idea what combination of words Harry would use; and when he sent 'BELIEVE,' it was a surprise."

Thus, mind-reading could not have been possible because Mrs. Houdini herself had not known the sequence of words which had been sealed in the envelope and locked within the vault of the Manufacturers' Trust Company.

To clinch the matter, Walter Winchell devoted his entire column of Saturday, January 19, 1929, to this letter written to him by Beatrice Houdini:

*Dear Mr. Walter Winchell:*
*This letter is not for publicity. I do not need publicity. I want to let Houdini's old friends know that I did not betray his trust.*

*I am writing this letter personally because I wish to tell you emphatically that I was no party to any fraud.*

*Now regarding the seance: For two years I have been praying to receive the message from my husband. Every day, for two years, I have received messages from all parts of the world. Had I wanted a publicity stunt I no doubt could have chosen any of these sensational messages. When I repudiated these messages, no one said a word excepting the writers who said I did not have the nerve to admit the truth.*

*When the real message, THE message that Houdini and I agreed upon, came to me, and I accepted it as the truth I was greeted with jeers. Why? Those who denounced the entire thing as a fraud claim that I had given Mr. A. Ford the message. If Mr. Ford said this I brand him a liar. Mr. Ford has since stoutly denied this ugly thing, and knowing him as well as I do, I prefer to believe Mr. Ford. Others say the message has been common property and known to them for some time. Why do they tell me this now, when they knew my heart was hungry for the true words of my husband!*

*The many stories told about me I have no way to tell to the world the truth or the untruth, for I have no paper at my beck and call, everyone has a different opinion of how the message was obtained. With all these different tales I would not even argue. However, when anyone accuses me of GIVING the words that my beloved husband and I labored so long to convince ourselves of the truth of communication, then I will fight and fight until the breath leaves my body.*

*If anyone claims I gave the code, I can only repeat they lie. Why should I want to cheat myself? I do not need publicity. I have no intention of going on the stage, or as some paper said, on a lecture tour. My husband made it possible for me to live in greatest comfort. I don't need to earn money. I have gotten the message I have been waiting for from my beloved, how, if not by spiritual aid, I do not know.*

*And now, after I told the world that I had received the true message, everyone seems to have known the code, yet never told me. They left it for Mr. Ford to tell me, and I am accused of giving the words. It's all so confusing. In conclusion may I say that God and Houdini and I know that I did not betray my trust. For the rest of the world I really ought not to care a hang, but somehow I do, therefore this letter. Forgive its length.*

*Sincerely yours,*
*Beatrice Houdini*

Beatrice Houdini died on February 18, 1943, bringing to a close one of the strangest debates in history. For some peculiar reason the controversy continues, although the truth of the affair seems conclusive. Arthur Ford had only this to say: "If asked to say on oath whether I know beyond the shadow of a doubt that I actually got the Houdini message, I could not do so on the basis of Mrs. Houdini's statement, and I can do no more."

*[Editor's Note: At the time of publication, this article was considered one of the most significant proofs of Spiritualism ever published. It is condensed from the booklet, "Houdini Unmasked," by Lydia Emery and compiled by R. G. Pressing. The booklet was published by Dale News, Inc., Lily Dale, NY, in 1947. The evidence has remained controversial. Allegations of fraud over this and other mediumship messages dogged Ford his entire life. Skeptics claimed he knew or was given the Houdini code, and that it had been previously published. The only ones who known the truth are Houdini and Beatrice.]*

FATE January 1950

# THE RETURN OF PATIENCE WORTH
## Harold O'Neal

While playing with a Ouija board in July 1913, Mrs. John H. Curran of St. Louis and her friend, Mrs. Emily Grant Hutchings, were suddenly astounded when the small wooden pointer began to glide from letter to letter spelling out: "Many moons ago I lived. Again I come. Patience Worth my name."

Startled, the ladies paused a moment to stare at one another. When they replaced their fingers on the pointer it rapidly spelled: "Wait, I will speak with thee. If thou shalt live, then so shall I."

Thus began the most remarkable case of Ouija board communication in the annals of psychic research. For a period of some 25 years Patience Worth dictated novels, epigrams and poetry through Mrs. Curran. A cynical newspaperman named Casper S. Yost investigated Mrs. Curran. Intent on exposing her as a fraud, he ended up a staunch believer in the phenomenon and wrote a book titled *Patience Worth* (1916).

Dr. Walter Franklin Prince, research officer of the American Society for Psychical Research, conducted the most thorough of all the investigations of the Patience Worth communications. And he too published a lengthy book presenting his conclusion: "Either our concept of what we call the subconscious must be radically altered so as to include potencies of which we hitherto have had no knowledge, or else some cause operating through but not originating in the subconsciousness of Mrs. Curran must be acknowledged."

When Mrs. Curran died in December 1937 the lively wit of Patience Worth was believed stilled – or so I thought until 1968.

First let it be understood that I am not a medium, nor is any member of my family – which consists of my wife and five children aged 14 through 24. On Christmas 1967, however, my youngest daughter gave me a Ouija board. To a fullfledged agnostic like myself, this seemed like a joke, but she begged me to try it.

By myself I could not get the pointer to budge so I asked my son Gary to work it with me. Just as skeptical as I, he jokingly agreed. But for the two of us the pointer began to move. "My name is Jacob," it spelled. From this small beginning came scads of information about the supposed previous lives of each member of the household. For several months we kept up the Ouija communications as an amusing pastime. Friends and neighbors often laughingly participated.

But Jacob often related events in ancient history that research proved were correct. This made me truly interested in the occult, and I purchased and read books by the dozens. Many of these referred to the story of Mrs. Curran and Patience Worth.

I finally concluded that my own doubts about a life after death would be resolved if I could contact Patience Worth.

"Do you know a Patience Worth?" I asked Jacob one night as we sat with the talking board. His reply was, "Never heard of her!" The possibility of contacting Patience Worth thus seemed remote, but the idea lingered.

One day while browsing in the game department of a large discount store I came across an "ESP Board," complete with a pendulum that was supposed to be swung above the letters on the board. I purchased this, but the pendulum seemed to take forever to spell out words. When I complained about this one of the girls suggested we use the pointer from the Ouija board.

It worked, bouncing joyfully over the middle fold of the board as it spelled. My daughter Kathy, by now a proficient Ouija operator even when blindfolded, took over the controls. The communicator gave her name as Patty Starry and related the horrifying tale of a 17-year-old girl caught alone near dark on a school ground in Colorado by an attacker who ravished and killed her. I asked, "Where are you now, Patty?" The reply was, "Heaven."

At this point one can truthfully state that we hesitated. In all our previous contacts the entities had told us they were in Limbo. After due commiseration with our unseen communicator I asked, "Do you by any chance know a Patience Worth, Patty?"

"She is my best friend," spelled the pointer.

"She's there?" I asked a bit breathlessly. The reply was slow in coming, almost as if something was trying to stop the movement of the pointer. Kathy looked up at me and asked, "Do you suppose she left?" Then the pointer slowly began to move again.

"Why do you wish to speak to Patience Worth?" it spelled.

"I admire her poetry which came through Mrs. Curran," I replied. "I would like her to recite for us."

The pointer hesitated then quickly swung to H, then E; H, then E; H, then E. It took a moment for the meaning of this to penetrate: "He, he, he!"

"She's giggling," said Kathy incredulously. "She's actually giggling."

The girlish enthusiasm for a compliment could be felt if not heard and we all broke into laughter. After another pause the pointer began to move rapidly as if a torrent of words needed to be expressed: "I am Patience Worth." The message seemed unnecessary as I thought I already had identified the communicator. Many months had passed since my initial desire to communicate with her; now finally she was here.

"Will you recite for us?" I asked. Without hesitation the pointer began to move between the letters. My wife Wanda, my daughter Karen and my son Michael each copied down letters as they were called out by Kathy: "OH GREAT ... " Divided into words this eventually came out as: "Oh, great God, thine wisdom is great, yet I have not believed thee. I will let thee tell me, now I must, for thou hast given me a great power which is love and also hath let me be loved. Thine wisdom is truly great and now I love thee forever and ever." Both the speed of dictation and the content of the message reminded me of Patience's dictation through Mrs. Curran.

To further test the identity of our new communicator I asked if she remembered Mrs. Curran. "I remember she," the board responded.

"Do you recall the first message you transmitted through the Ouija board to Mrs. Curran?" I asked.

The pointer rapidly spelled out: "Many moons ago I lived. Again I come."

This correct response was impressive in view of the fact that Kathy, who was operating the board, did not know these words. In fact, I was the only one present who did know the correct response. As a skeptical friend pointed out, it could have been telepathy between Kathy and me. But if this were true, I wonder why I never am able to think Kathy into helping her mother with the housework!

When I asked Patience whether she had liked Mrs. Curran, the board replied, "That woman!" When I said I understood Mrs. Curran eventually was able to put aside the Ouija and receive Patience's messages through her mind, the pointer fairly flew across the board: "I D I D N O T R E S I GHTTH ROUGHHE R MINUT EB RAIN!" which breaks down into "I did not resight through her minute brain!"

"If you had such little respect for Mrs. Curran," I asked, "why did you choose her Ouija board to communicate through?"

"Well," she replied, "I was anxious to have one."

As word of our Ouija communications spread we often found our dining table surrounded by interested friends. I began to realize how Mrs. Curran must have felt when she asked investigator Walter Franklin Prince, "Won't you remove for good from the minds of the public that I am a medium with a gold shingle and trances?"

On one occasion the visitors included some young married couples, acquaintances who came to see the strange kooks who thought they could communicate with spirits of the dead. After much hilarity we were persuaded to break out the communication board. Patience Worth graciously acknowledged the introductions. We told her that one of the young men, Kenneth M., just had been discharged from army service.

"Will you recite something appropriate, Patience?" I asked.

Quickly the pointer spelled out: "Sons of liberty, O God, forgiveth them, for they are not yet believers in thine noble strength but I fear shall soon be."

The ex-soldier pursed his lips thoughtfully and then asked, "Patience, can you tell me something that only I know?"

Without hesitation the pointer began to describe a vicious barracks fight at the army base in Fort Lee, Virginia. A knife had been pulled on Ken. The young man's face paled visibly as this account was given. Patience later apologized for embarrassing him in front of the other guests. He told me later the incident had occurred exactly as Patience had described it.

In her message through Mrs. Curran, Patience Worth made comments that seemingly repudiate reincarnation. Statements made through our ESP board, however, seem to support this concept, although the first such message came at a time when we weren't asking about reincarnation as such.

I had asked, "Please, Patience, give in 15 words or less the reason for immortality."

The pointer glided rapidly back and forth across the board: "Thee cannot be good enough to have only one life on this plane of existence."

At a later session Patience was more explicit and announced she had had five earth lives. I naturally assumed that her life as Patience Worth had been her most recent but when I asked her one day she replied, "I last lived as Nora Fleming in Scotland, 1828." Unfortunately, this is all the information she gave about this alleged life and it thus would be impossible to verify that such a person lived. I was puzzled that she preferred to identify herself with a much older incarnation than that of Nora Fleming. Her explanation was simple: "I liked the life of Patience Worth. I learned from it."

Some of the messages from Patience hinted that she had a collaborator during her contacts with Mrs. Curran. Early in 1969 I asked her, "Who helped you write through Mrs. Curran?"

"Hannah Pringle," was the reply.

"Where is Hannah?"

"Limbo, if she hasn't been reborn." This suggested the idea of trying to contact Hannah Pringle through the Ouija board. After much

93

conversation with other entities, I finally did contact Hannah, a wild extrovert who called me Charles and intimated that we had been more than a little close in merry old England in the 1500s. Alas, my memory does not extend that far back, and I am unable to verify Hannah's statements.

I informed Hannah that her old friend Patience Worth wished to say hello. The conversation from the Ouija board grew spirited as Hannah recalled to us her old friend. She wondered if she could speak directly to Patience herself. This posed a problem. Those in Limbo seemed to speak only through the Ouija board while those in Heaven used the ESP board. We finally decided to try with the two boards side by side, with my left hand on the pointer of the Ouija and my right on the pointer of the ESP board.

The two pointers circled for a while without spelling anything, as if they were testing the automatist. Shortly the hair on my arms raised and I felt an electric-like charge course through my body. The pointers began to move rapidly.

"How are thee, Hannah?" asked Patience.

"I have missed thee," replied Hannah.

The pace grew hectic. As fast as the pointers could move on the respective boards Patience and Hannah spelled messages to each other, often at the same time. I raised my hands until only the middle fingers still made contact. If only one pointer was spelling the other would spin under my fingers and seem to look at the other board. Perhaps the ghostly friends were seeing each other; they never said.

After repeated requests to slow down, the pointers eventually did so. As the two communicators supposedly had collaborated on literary works through Mrs. Curran, I asked if they would communicate something through me. After considerable discussion between them they decided to write a play entitled "The Unhappy Child." We had managed to receive only the first scene when a visitor commented, "Well, it's not very good." Apparently indignant over this, Hannah and Patience refused to continue.

During the first half of 1969 circumstances prevented me from continuing with the boards. When I finally was able to resume in July we made contact, on Patience's board, with an entity named Mobley with whom we had talked before.

"Where is Patience?" I asked.

"Reborn!" was the cryptic reply. Then he explained that Patience had been reborn as a beautiful baby girl to a couple in Connecticut on June 17, 1969. He told us the last name of the couple which I agreed not to publish.

Permit me to say, in conclusion, that my attitude toward this life has been changed considerably by this experience. For, if this is only one phase of everlasting existence then Patience was right when she admonished, "Be thouself; love each other; ye shall meet again."

FATE November 1976

# LORD DOWDING'S RETURN
## J.J. Snyder

In the summer of 1940, the British Royal Air Force Fighter Command won the Battle of Britain. Fighting overwhelming odds, they saved their country from Nazi domination by defeating the German Luftwaffe in a series of hard-fought air engagements over the threatened island.

The head of Fighter Command during those desperate times was Air Chief Marshal Hugh Dowding, a long-time pilot and a brilliant air combat strategist. One of Britain's earliest airmen, Dowding began flying in 1913 and had been wounded on a combat mission during World War I.

That spring, Dowding had faced down Winston Churchill and, after a heated argument, persuaded the prime minister not to send the few remaining fighter aircraft of the RAF to France in what would have been a fruitless attempt to reinforce the British Expeditionary Force. Even though Dowding's strategy eventually led to England's victory in the Battle of Britain, Churchill still held bitter feelings toward him. Soon after the Nazi air blitz faltered, the prime minister, with the help of Dowding's detractors, saw to it that the Air Chief Marshal was removed from his post.

Dowding was disappointed that political animosity had removed any further opportunity of serving his country, but he bore Churchill and the others no ill will. In retirement, he turned to exploring and writing on a subject that had long been of interest to him – communicating with the dead. He was especially drawn to making contact with "his boys" – RAF pilots and air crew who had made the supreme sacrifice for king and country.

Dowding's two books, *Many Mansions* and *Lychgate,* which present hard evidence for the continuity of all life, are classics of survival literature. During and after the war, he traveled throughout the country, speaking about his many contacts with those in the astral realms. In these appearances, he offered what he considered irrefutable proof of existence beyond the physical life.

Dowding cautioned his audiences not to accept his evidence solely on the basis of his fame. He told them instead to employ their own reason and intellect when examining the possibility of life beyond physical death. He thought that any rational, unbiased person would come to see the truth on the strength of the verifiable facts.

In 1970, after a long and distinguished mortal life, Lord Dowding departed for the etheric world he knew so well. Since his passing, he has communicated several times with the physical level he left behind. His contact on September 15, 1996 is perhaps the most compelling.

## An anniversary appearance

The date is important, for it marked the culmination of the 1940 Nazi air assault against Britain. It was on this day that the forces of Fighter Command were stretched to their thinnest. September 15 – Battle of Britain Day – is celebrated throughout the United Kingdom. It is surely no coincidence that Dowding chose to appear on that date 56 years later at a session conducted by the Noah's Ark Society (NAS).

The NAS is a British organization dedicated to promoting and developing physical mediumship as a means of proving the survival of personality beyond death. To this end the Society has sponsored numerous events to initiate and verify communication between the physical and etheric planes. Lord Dowding's materialization at the NAS seminar at Cardiff, Wales, was one of the best-documented in the history of these events. Dowding made his appearance through Colin Fry, a gifted psychic medium. Although the proceedings were held in total darkness (a condition mediums feel is more conducive to materializations than a lighted room), Dowding reportedly was seen, touched and spoken to by many people.

*Lord Dowding.*

Although hearing voices and making visual contact with inhabitants of etheric regions are rather common, full physical materialization, during which mortals are able to touch and feel the etherians, is relatively rare. Even so, it has been studied extensively and verified by a number of respected scientists, including Sir William Crookes, Professor Charles Richet, and Sir John Logie Baird. Modern researchers are also conducting experiments to learn more about this phenomenon.

Reports submitted by scientists who have investigated these events indicate that full materialization is usually accomplished through a specially talented medium – one who can enable the finer subatomic structure and higher frequencies of the discarnates to coalesce into the coarser vibrations of this mortal plane. When this occurs, the etherian becomes visible and may be touched and communicated with by those present. Spontaneous materializations – occurring with no medium present – have also been recorded, usually involving people who were close to each other on the physical plane.

At his own request, Colin Fry was securely tied and strapped to his chair, which was located in a cabinet constructed of black cloth. Tying and strapping the medium is a common practice in materialization experiments, which can be open to charges of fraud and deceit, especially when conducted in total darkness. Binding the medium tightly and noting and photographing the position and type of knots and straps before and after the session provide evidence that the medium has not moved while the lights are out.

A recording of the session was made by the NAS. At the beginning, Dowding can be heard uttering the words "jolly nice" a number of times. Although he was in his late eighties when he transitioned, his voice has the timbre of a middle-aged man.

## Lord Dowding appears

After touching several of the participants, Dowding tapped and rattled the two microphones placed on either side of the medium. Then, in an imitation of Lord Haw Haw, the notorious English traitor whose propaganda broadcasts were transmitted to Britain during the war, he repeated "Germany calling, Germany calling" several times. These were the opening words of Haw Haw's broadcasts.

Those in the audience were unaware that the personality which had just materialized was Lord Dowding. He at first declined to reveal his identity. Urged to make himself known, he finally stated, "Probably some of you know of me ... Dowding." He continued shaking hands.

When told that he might write a message on a piece of paper that had been placed on the floor, he declared that the last time he wrote on the floor was at the age of three, when he drew pictures of birds in flight. Then, seeming to express regret for his part in a horrible war, he said that "to learn to soar in the skies, to be free like a bird, is an honorable thing. But the only things that birds drop on us don't blow people to pieces... and that is my shame."

Dowding was then questioned as to whether those who caused him to be removed from his post, many of whom are now presumably discarnate, had become aware of what they had done.

"They probably are," he said, "but it doesn't make a damn bit of difference now. Offended sensibilities are in the end only bloody arrogance. If you can behave better toward those who are at fault, it makes you a better person, doesn't it? Above all else have honor. If you behave honorably toward other people, it really doesn't matter how they behave toward you."

He continued moving through the crowd, touching those present and shaking hands. He recognized one woman and noted that he had spoken with her many times before.

Having known Dowding during the war, the woman confirmed the apparition's identity. She said that he displayed his keen sense of humor, of which she had firsthand knowledge.

Her statement is important, since only those who were close to Dowding are aware of this facet of his personality. Although his public image was that of a stiff, correct military officer – his RAF nickname was "Stuffy" – his friends knew and appreciated his quick, dry wit. Upon parting with the lady, Dowding kissed her hand, a sound clearly audible to the gathering.

In his closing words, Dowding once again voiced deep regret for the tragedy of the Second World War.

"Don't look to past victories," he said. "Pain, suffering and unnecessary bloodshed, even one drop of blood or one life lost to our side is no victory – just awful, hideous defeat. I'm sorry I couldn't touch you all, but I hope that I can touch you with my heart."

In answer to a "God bless you" from a member of the audience, he replied, "No, God bless you, my friends. You are the ones still in the battle. I would have rather played a more valuable role in a more honorable game." He then said goodbye and left.

One of the many present who shook hands with Lord Dowding was NAS committee member Geoff Hughes, who noted that the etheric

Air Marshal shook his hand "quite hard." Dowding also walked behind the back row and patted people on the shoulder as he passed.

The large number of witnesses who observed this remarkable event, and the similarity of their accounts of what occurred, as well as the audio recording, seem to make it one of the most convincing materializations on record. It is hoped that Lord Dowding will see fit to return to this mortal level and perhaps allow himself to be photographed by infrared camera and videotape, which should be compatible with the total darkness requirement for materialization. If this happens, and the tapes and photos match witnesses' testimony, it will be a telling refutation of those who deny the continuity of life.

*J. J. Snyder: Agricultural pilot and aviation writer in paranormal research.*

FATE August 1998

# PAINTINGS FROM ANOTHER WORLD
## Gerry Annette Petersen

It is an exciting experience to find oneself painting the faces and forms of those who have pre-existed. There is no deeper thrill than seeing the portrait of a former physical being of an ancient day develop beneath one's fingertips! About four years ago I surprisingly developed this form of mediumship.

Some years ago, with friends who are psychics, I experimented with mental telepathy, using it to communicate with visitants from the beyond. At this time I was clairvoyantly impelled to draw crude likenesses of some of the Etheric Teachers who were instructing us. Clairaudiently, we acquired information pertaining to our past lives. However, these psychic meetings came to an end when my family and I moved away.

During the next two years I spent most of my spare time acting as amanuensis to many spirit souls. When this period of transcribing terminated abruptly I found I had a tremendous urge to study the human aura. I was often inspired to sketch personalized auras that were symbolically beautiful in their vivid designs. I composed them for loved ones and friends, and each aura that I fashioned was as different as were the individuals for whom I drew them.

*Leonardo da Vinci was one of the spirit guides who inspired paintings such as this.*

Although the person might be miles away, by focusing my power of concentration upon them, I could place my consciousness in close contact with theirs. This immediately established a strong channel of telepathic vibrations. Thus, clairvoyantly, I obtained the design of the auric envelope which portrayed the spiritual attributes of each soul. I used water color pencils to portray the auras in exquisite jewel-like colors. I worked very rapidly and, strangely, during the composition of these auras some of the previous existences of the individual were revealed to me.

Soon I became aware of the vibratory presence of other Invisibles. They imbued me with the desire to sketch symbolic, cosmic flowers which I had seen on several occasions while astrally projected. Each flower had a symbolic title and an explanation of its spiritual import.

*This flower symbolizes the unfoldment of a soul. The radiance around it denotes the spiritual attributes of a person.*

Further auric decorations evolved when I surrounded these symmetrical blossoms with delicate, prismatic radiations of auric lights which unified themselves into brilliant patterns of design.

A short time later I was directed to reproduce these designs in oils. The only art training I have ever received was in high school. I know nothing of the technique of oil painting.

During an experimental period of two weeks a kindly soul who called himself Henry Bach guided me in the blending of the numerous shades of colors necessary for reproducing the flowers in the tones previously employed. After diligently devoting nearly all my spare time to this learning I decided that I was ready to begin painting. With the passage of the months I progressed more quickly with the new medium. I would like to acknowledge, in the order in which they came to me, those besides Henry Bach who assisted me during this period. They were: Master Sing Li, of ancient China; Onatele, an American Indian maid; Pierre Redoute, of France; and Ahmid, of ancient Persia.

As the year drew to a close I received an entirely new impression which I acted upon by securing larger canvases for my future assignments. At the same time, I did not possess the slightest inkling of what my Teachers had in store for me.

The day came when I first sat at my larger canvas with the impression to sketch a life-size head of Ahmid of Persia. Although I had sensed his presence countless times I had never seen him clairvoyantly. Imagine my astonishment at seeing him take form on canvas! My hands literally flew and in an unbelievably short time the sketch was complete and ready for painting!

I had begun by sketching the eyes first which, incidentally, sometimes appear larger than normal eyes. I recalled that I employed this identical method to draw the Etheric Teachers who had tutored my friends and me. This procedure differs from the usual academic art instructions.

One possible explanation for such a method is that the eyes are often thought of as mirrors which reflect the soul. Therefore, I believe this same principle could apply to those souls existing on another plane. By using this procedure, I achieved the expression of the eyes desired by my Teachers and I also was able to obtain further impressions from them concerning the other features, mode of attire and background.

*Prince Faroud Ra of ancient Egypt. Done while in trance.*

After I mixed my colors for Ahmid's skin and features and commenced to paint I felt myself falling into a semi-trance condition. I had experienced this phase of mediumship previously but under far different circumstances. I perceived that a strong outside force was taking control of my hand and brush, guiding them with skill. In a very short time the skin and features were painted. I was pleased with their lifelike appearance. I was permitted to paint the costume and background without the trance condition prevailing.

After finishing *The Young Rajah* I completed other portraits and noticed that I was becoming a more proficient instrument for my Etheric tutors. We enjoyed a friendly relationship, one that proved deeply beneficial to me in numerous ways.

In succession, I created the following images in oil: Emir, Bedouin Chieftain, of Arabia; Tee/ii Pu/ti, Inca of Peru; and Prince Faroud Ra of ancient Egypt.

I have had the impression of guidance from two other teachers for my portrait work. They are Master Leonardo Da Vinci and Pierre Puvis De Chavannes. I am eternally grateful for all the kind souls who have allowed me to be an instrument for this type of inspirational work. These Etheric beings, who have descended from other cosmic spheres, always have been kind and patient with me and they have never for one moment infringed upon my personal life.

At the present I consider myself a novice in this expanding field of psychic endeavor. There are others far more adept than I who are doing work in this same category. I sincerely hope that I shall be permitted to continue to explore new vistas under the kind tutelage of the patient entities whose creative destinies have been linked with mine.

FATE September 1953

# SPIRITS IN THE CHAIR
## Whitley Dresser

The dead live. They can communicate with us, know how we're doing, and are interested in our well-being. You can prove this to yourself, as 18 people did in a psychic development class on a sultry July night in 1989. They engaged in a group experiment to "talk" to deceased loved ones and came up with enough factual material to convince themselves that they accomplished just that.

The event took place at *Rainbow's End*, a tiny New Age bookstore next to a pizza parlor in Centerbrook, Connecticut. The shop is owned by Muriel McIntyre, a short, cheerful lady who obviously loves what she's doing. It's been her practice to have New Age teachers come to her shop to conduct classes in astrology, psychic development and the like.

I was the instructor on this muggy, mid-summer evening, and proposed a group communication experiment to prove a point: You don't need a professional medium to get in touch with those who have gone on.

We placed an empty chair in the center of the circle, and then asked for a volunteer to offer the name of a relative or close friend who had recently died. No further information of any kind was allowed. The purpose of the chair was simply to help us to focus our thoughts. We would silently repeat the name and try to imagine the invisible spirit entity named taking a seat. Then we would hold a silent "conversation" with whomever we sensed was there. To a casual observer the sight of 18 adults holding silent communion with a vacant chair would be ridiculous – until we began to share what we had picked up.

Because of the personal and somewhat sensitive nature of what came through this mental communication, we have changed some names. In many ways, it is like listening to a private phone conversation between intimate friends. Keep in mind that the group was composed of ordinary people, mostly women, as is normal in this type of gathering. Many men are more trapped in conventional thinking than their female counterparts. The details of the communications were likewise ordinary and intimate. No Cleopatras or Napoleons here.

## "She liked baseball"

The first name offered was Ida May McGinley. After about five quiet minutes a tentative, somewhat embarrassed voice broke the silence. "I see her as blonde, she's about 27, I think. Then she told me she was 57."

"I think she's older, perhaps late 50s," said another. There is something about a red brick building. I see a garden. I keep seeing a garden."

"She liked baseball. Loved the color aqua. I see her in a blue dress." The group was getting into it.

"She was blonde, heavy, with a round face. Her hair is pulled back. She's wearing an apron over a housedress. She worked hard during her life. She had three children. She died of cancer?"

"I see lace. What about lace? Did she like lace?"

"I think she had five children. I think her hair was grey."

## The real Ida May

Then Joanne, whose mother was Ida May McGinley, gave us the facts: Ida was blonde, heavy, with a broad face. She lived in a red brick house. She worked as a cook in a convalescent home and loved to garden. She died at

75 years of age of a heart attack, not cancer, and had Alzheimer's Disease. She bore five children. She loved blue, and her husband was a baseball player. Her all-time favorite dress was aqua blue with a lace collar.

Joanne added that she seemed to hear her mother say to her, "I love you. Be happy. Have a good life."

Perhaps the key here was the love of baseball. It is this kind of information that we find so interesting, the unexpected details of people's lives – their likes and dislikes – that don't fit any stereotype. She was nothing dramatic or awe-inspiring, just a lady who worked hard, raised five kids, loved her garden, and had a baseball player as a husband. And she's still able to tell us about herself.

## Two unborn children

The next person called to "sit" in the chair we'll call Doris Macklin. The class went into meditation again, then came the comments:

"I get the smell of apples. Lots of energy."

"Dorothy was tall, dark haired, dark eyed. She loved the beach. I see her walking along the beach. She is looking at the water."

"There is a large, white house, like those places you see in Newport, Rhode Island. There is something about California. I think she lived in California, too. She loved music. Played the piano perhaps."

"She loved pretty clothes, jewelry, liked to decorate her home. She was an intellectual, loved to read. Was she a teacher?"

"She was very beautiful, tall, elegant. Wanted to be in the theater. Loved to entertain. Go out to dinner. Was outwardly happy but was in a lot of inner pain. She says we should not try to hide things from people. She was unhappily married. Something about an alcoholic. She had four children. There was cancer. She smoked a lot. Did she die of cancer?"

"She shows us two children, babies; they are not yet born. She brings them to us. She wants them placed in a spiritual light. She is concerned about their being brought into a spiritual light. I don't understand."

## The real Doris

Lynn Moore gave us this information about Doris: Doris was her sister. She had lived in California, as well as Rhode Island and Connecticut. She did reside for a time in a large, white house on the beach. She was five feet nine inches tall, had dark hair and eyes and was very elegant. She loved music but did not play an instrument. She married an alcoholic, a union which was very unhappy, and the marriage ended. She smoked heavily, had cancer, which finally killed her, but it was not cancer of the lungs. The significance of the smell of apples was not identified.

One of the most significant parts of the entire communication with the entity Doris was her concern about the two unborn infants. Lynn Moore knew that one of her sister's daughters was at this time about three months pregnant. What Lynn did not know was that Doris' son had a wife who was also pregnant.

The two sisters, Lynn and Doris, had a kind of standing joke between them about matters of religion. Doris had been a devout Catholic, rejecting all notions of reincarnation and the like, while Lynn was probing deeply into New Age philosophies and concepts, and questioning her own Catholic views. Lynn had even dragged the reluctant Doris to a psychic but made no headway. The joke was that if the strictly Catholic Doris died first, she would return and tell Lynn she had been wrong.

We felt that when Doris showed us the two unborn babies and asked that they be brought into the light of spirit, this was an admission to her sister that she wanted these babies to be brought up in a less restrictive religious atmosphere, "the spiritual light."

Lynn was unaware at the time that there were two pregnant women in Doris' family, so mental telepathy from Lynn was ruled out. This appears to be a crucial point. One could argue that the information being transmitted by "spirits" to members of the group could be nothing more than some kind of mental communication from the one who offered the name to us. But when unknown information comes through, facts which are only later verified, this no longer holds. The group members who volunteer names unanimously agreed that most of the details that come through were unexpected, even surprising.

The fact that this woman in spirit was concerned about the welfare of as yet unborn children – her grandchildren – and that she was able to bring them into our awareness is astonishing enough. What has far more implications is the notion that these souls were destined for birth into a family, and to specific mothers, and that the spirit knew this in the early months of the physical pregnancy of those mothers.

## Golf, golf, golf

Finally, one Bob Fairchild (not his real name) was "placed" in the chair. And again, the comments came from around the room:

"He was young when he died. He was very generous with money. Liked people. Loved sports. I hear golf, golf, golf. He was sandy-haired."

"There is something silver. Something like a belt buckle. I can't quite understand what it is."

"There was some kind of boating accident on a lake. Did he die in a boating accident?"

"He is concerned about his wife. Is she drinking too much? He seems worried about her."

"He died at the age of 32 of a heart attack."

The details then given were these: Bob was a policeman. The "something silver, like a belt buckle" was the badge he was trying to show us. He was gregarious, loved people and a good time. He loved sports. He did not die of a boating accident but was on vacation at a lake when stricken with a fatal heart attack. He was 32 years old when he died. His wife is having a very difficult time accepting his untimely death and she seems to be drinking heavily.

## Where does the information come from?

In each case, there was no question in the mind of the person who volunteered the name that the material was authentic. There was enough identifying material to convince us all that there was something valid going on here. Keep in mind that most of the group were strangers to each other and to me, the leader. The information received was not known and could not have been known to anyone but the one who volunteered the name.

This experiment has been done on several different occasions with other people with equally evidential results. In some cases, group members have picked up information which was so odd that it would be difficult, if not impossible, to imagine someone dreaming it up.

One night in another session, two or three in the group received pictures of oil drums, and several people commented on the smell of oil that seemed to be in the air. It turned out that the young man who was in spirit in the chair was killed in an oil rig explosion. Since nobody except his sister (who gave us his name) knew anything of the individual, such images, we believe, could come from only one source – the deceased.

We have discovered that often our spirits will show themselves at different ages – we have had perceptions of the same person, say in their 20s, and then again in their 60s or 70s. We also found that other close relatives in spirit will sometimes accompany those who "sit" in the chair, and often have picked up information about them as well.

## How you can do this experiment

Can this experiment be duplicated, and if so, are there any dangers? To the first part of the question we can offer an unqualified yes. To the second, there are some safeguards that should be observed.

Earlier I said that newly deceased loved ones or close friends are the most likely respondents to this kind of thing. Recently deceased means within a year or two. I feel that those not long in spirit often wish to communicate with family and are still emotionally close. As time wears on they appear to have other things to do and other places to go. In one or two cases, where those contacted have been dead for a long time, we have sensed an unwillingness to be bothered by the concerns of friends or relatives in the flesh. In one instance we felt distinct resistance from the entities to being called to the chair in the center of the room.

Loved ones or close friends are preferable in this kind of experiment, since the kind of intimate details of life information is readily available, and thus offers better proof than some national or historical figure, whose biography could be common knowledge.

It is important to realize that it is very unlikely that someone – a ghost – will dramatically appear in the chair. I have found that many people are very apprehensive about what might take place in this kind of a session. We have all heard ghost stories and the leader of such an experiment should take time to demystify the proceedings.

While mentally calling the name, class members try, as I have described, to "see" the deceased, developing a kind of silent conversation with whomever they visualize. After about five to 10 minutes of the kind of questioning that you might do with a stranger you wanted to know more about, the leader asks if anyone has picked up some information. Questions are along the lines of identification: What does the spirit look like? What was its occupation during life? Where did the spirit live? How many children did they have? What was the manner of death? Was the life happy or sad? And so forth.

Of utmost importance in the whole procedure is the attainment of the quiet, meditative condition by the group, thus bypassing the constant internal chatter and critical evaluation of our usual state of mind. This "conversation" is not a verbal, left brain kind of thing that we're used to in our ordinary interaction with people. We must utilize our intuitive, nonverbal intelligence, or right-brain capacity.

The language of the spirit is through mind-to-mind contact: mental images will flow through your consciousness and feelings will arise. You may "hear" words, but not audibly. You may smell an aroma like apples, or oil, for instance. It is a kind of free-flowing excursion of the imagination, where thoughts, images and sensations just happen. The key word here is to "allow." Let it happen. Don't edit. Throwing out a scene that flashes through your head because it doesn't make sense will short-circuit the process. This takes some getting used to, since most of us are so oriented to language and linear, time-space objectivity.

## What are the risks?

Are there any risks involved? Can you, or should you, do it? In group work, I always offer a kind of affirmation or prayer, if you will, prior to going into the meditative state. We also ask permission. This affirmation sets up the "intent," or "mental vibration" that attracts those in spirit. When the intent is one of love and based upon the desire to acquire knowledge and communication, I feel that this will allow only those who are genuinely concerned with our welfare to come into our consciousness. Since this appears to be the case in all my experiences, I can see no risk.

At the close of the session, we go into a clearing exercise, just to eliminate any lingering effect that might exist. This consists of visualizing a white light moving from above the crown of the head to the feet, and then offering thanks to those who have come to help and guide us.

The attitude of the participants seems to be important. You must be relaxed, have fun and enjoy the experience. Otherwise, attaining the meditative state – the alpha brain-wave condition of relaxation and mental awareness – is nearly impossible and there will be no communication. The group should be accustomed to the art of meditation and allowing the images to flow.

## Why contact spirits?

Contact with spirits is important. If we become convinced that we are actually in the presence of conscious, thinking, aware beings who have died and that they can and do communicate with us, then it is obvious that we are going to have certain ideas about death and dying.

The process of change in the national consciousness has had a good start with the publication of the many studies about the near-death experience. Books by such eminent figures as Dr. Elisabeth Kübler-Ross, including her widely known *On Death and Dying*, Dr. Kenneth Ring's *Life at Death*, Dr. Raymond R. Moody's *Life After Life*, and many others are based upon solid research done with persons who have experienced resuscitation after being pronounced clinically dead. Valuable as these accounts are, they are still the experiences of someone else.

Not everyone is going to have a near-death episode, but personal contact with a mother or someone close who has died is going to change attitudes about death.

## Spirit communication without a medium

Many people look upon the psychic or medium as either something awesome or a fraud. Neither attitude is appropriate. There is nothing that the professional psychic can do that you can't. It is simply a matter of training the intuitive, right-brained awareness to perceive inputs normally cast out as products of too much chili for lunch. There is fraud in the marketplace, whether in selling psychic services or selling shoes. But not every shoe salesman is a crook, and neither is every psychic.

Small groups of sincere seekers into the realms of consciousness heretofore hidden to us by our education, training and so-called scientific attitudes will produce that kind of experiential knowledge that will enable you to say, "I know."

Once you say that, your life is forever changed.

FATE August 1991

# HOW TO RUN A HOME SEANCE
## Dr. W. D. Chesney

The power of certain mediums to break through the veil and put us into communication with those we have loved and lost is unquestioned nowadays by many of us. I know it is possible to hold conversations with those who are living but invisible to our eyes – if certain conditions are supplied. And these conditions can be supplied.

Every reputable medium I have known has discovered his or her psychic gifts in home seances. The Eddys, the Davenports, the Crandons, the Currans of Patience Worth fame, all discovered their psychic capabilities in home seances, in their own "upper rooms."

Abraham Lincoln found that he was mediumistic in seances held in his Springfield home before he ran for the Presidency. Nettie Colburn Maynard, the medium who served Mr. Lincoln up to the time of his transition, developed her mediumship in her "upper room" in Bolton, Connecticut, a number of years before the Hydesville manifestations in the "upper room" of the Fox family.

From the dawn of recorded history – possibly even longer – man has wanted a private spot where he may rest and meditate. He may wish to be alone to commune with his God. Or he may take Christ's words to heart, that where two or three are gathered together in His name, He will be in the midst of them.

It must be clear to us that this "upper room" is now a symbol only, of privacy and safety. Earlier in our history a literal "upper room" was necessary because there a man could see his enemy approach before his enemy saw him. During the time that no man, outside the priesthood, could have or read the Holy Bible, it was essential that the layman read his forbidden book in an "upper room" so that sufficient time was available to hide the Book in case of interruption.

During the Pagan persecutions of the early Christians an "upper room" was still a necessity. Sometimes it was a loft over a ground floor; sometimes it was a cave or a catacomb, but symbolically an "upper room" none the less.

An "upper room" is necessary to many persons as a protection against the jibes and jeers of unbelieving friends and neighbors. But today, all over the world, families are holding seances and developing every phase of psychic phenomena – automatic writing, independent writing, direct and indirect voices, materialization and spiritual healings.

It is safe to assume that our departed friends and relatives are as anxious as we to break through the veil and to prove that there is no death. It was the spirits of those called "dead" who opened the way when the Foxes and Colburns were ignorant of any modus operandi for communicating with them.

The most important step is to eliminate the greatest curse of mankind – fear. One should be positive with Victor Hugo that, "The tomb is not a blind alley. It is a broad highway that closes on the twilight and opens on the eternal dawn of immortality."

In the early 1880s a number of Abe Lincoln's old friends used to visit Father's offices in Kansas City and Topeka and, as every one of them knew of Mr. Lincoln's psychic experiences and his profound belief in psychic communication between the seen and the unseen, it logically followed that they were interested in home seances.

We had about the largest house in Topeka – 17 rooms, no bathrooms in those days. There were seven rooms on the first and second stories and one immense room on the third floor. My own grandfather was a red-hot Methodist and opposed to research in psychic matters, so my father and the others decided to use the large room at the top of the house as their "upper room." A large table and about 20 chairs were carried up there. An old reed organ that Father had sent out from Springfield, Illinois in the mid-1870s was there also.

As far as we knew not one of those comprising the circle ever had been mediumistic. The following information should be carefully considered for it will help to enhance the results and eliminate the dangers of your own home seances. May I say first that silly questions, to silly (earthbound) spirits, get silly answers. The opposite is equally true: sensible people, asking for sensible information from developed spirits, will bring sensible replies which positively prove that friends you thought dead still live and love.

Bear in mind that the act of physically dying does not confer a gold crown, gold slippers, gold harp and angelic wings on the spirit of a good man. Nor is the spirit of an evil man automatically presented with a trident, cloven hooves, horns and the wings of a bat. His spirit is just exactly the same in every way as it was one minute before his heart stopped beating in his physical body.

It is a spiritual law that good attracts good. Evil attracts evil. Therefore, in seances held with respectable, earnest truth seekers and a medium controlled by good entities thus attracted, the information is good and, within limitations imposed on the psychic which are comparable to a radio or television set, the information is dependable. Your radio or TV does not give uniformly good reception – neither does a medium.

An even dozen friends and old Lincoln cronies assembled in our "upper-room" on Lincoln Street, Topeka, that first night.

We made a complete circle by clasping the hands of the persons next to us. My sister Mary played the old reed organ. I, being just a kid, was an innocent, ignorant participant. The kerosene lamp (we had no electric lights in our homes in those halcyon days) was turned quite low. Mary played church hymns on the organ to accompany the voices of the sitters. It was a rather warm evening as we began but before very long we began to feel currents of cold air where there should not have been any.

One very large man named Sain sat with us and was about the last man on earth one would consider psychic. His education was sketchy – I doubt if he had attended school five years in his life. But at the end of 30 minutes small, brilliant lights began dashing around the room and, without further ado, Sain was controlled and delivered one of the finest oratorial efforts I ever have heard. The entity, speaking through Sain's vocal organs, identified himself as the great preacher and temperance lecturer, Lorenzo Dow. I know that Sain used words he himself had never heard before.

After this lecture some close relatives of various sitters gave convincing evidence of their spiritual identity by presenting evidence not known to the sitters, but which later was checked and found to be true.

During our third meeting, two weeks later, a voice absolutely unlike the voice of Sain addressed my father as Ez (short for Ezra) and identified himself as Abraham Lincoln. I heard more than one of those who had known Honest Abe in life whisper, "That sure is Abe Lincoln's voice." And it seems to me, as I recall the messages subsequently received, that from that time on I knew the grand character of the martyred President, Abe Lincoln, as no one can now know him.

The voice of Lincoln said to Father, "Ez, Major Ritchie is here with me and he wants you to tell John and Hale (Major Ritchie's sons) not to attempt to force the return of the college grant because the college means a whole lot more to Kansas than to bear my name, Lincoln College."

A fairly long conversation was carried on with Father who identified the voice, the wisdom, the intonation and the character as that of his old mentor, Abe Lincoln. After the circle had broken up for the evening Father gave us the history of the matter to which Lincoln's spirit referred.

Major Ritchie had accumulated a large acreage on the southwest side of Topeka. Later he set aside some of this property to provide a perpetual fund to a college to be known for all time as Lincoln College. When hard times came on and it appeared that the college could no longer survive, a wealthy miller offered to advance a large sum of money if the school name was changed to Washburn College. The Ritchie boys, John and Hale, came to Father and asked him to sue for the return of the endowment because of the breach of contract. In fact, right at the time of the seance my father was making a study of the situation pursuant to suing the college corporation.

Father accepted this message at face value and urged the Ritchie boys not to sue. In fact, he refused to sue, making the Ritchie boys his enemies for life. They did not sue but went behind Father's back and settled a damage suit with the Kansas, Nebraska & Dakota railroad in order to avoid Father's already earned fee.

It has been said, with some basis, that Lincoln wrote and issued the Emancipation Proclamation under the urgings of the spirit of Daniel Webster. And Carl Schurz, United States Senator from Missouri, admitted in writing that Lincoln's spirit voice, heard at a home seance in Philadelphia, predicted correctly that he would hold that office despite the fact that Schurz at the time was a resident of Wisconsin. I knew Carl Schurz and can swear that this is true.

When we first began to hold seances in our Topeka home back in the 1880s my mother, a strict Methodist, was not very enthusiastic about it. But as she sat in the circle she had the most urgent desire which she resisted for a long time – to pick up a pencil. The guides had told both my mother and my sister Mary that they could do automatic writing and later they did just that. The information that came through them was always factually correct.

One day, without saying a word, Father simply handed Mother a very old planchette, with ball bearings, to my best recollection, and Mother took her old lap board, placed a large sheet of wrapping paper on it, set the planchette on the paper, the fingers of her right hand on the planchette and almost immediately messages came through from deceased relatives and friends.

When Mother sat down to the planchette nothing could drive us younger children from the house. It surely kept us out of mischief for hours at a time. And let no one tell you we did not have juvenile delinquency in those days too. One of the marvels of Mother's mediumship was that, using the planchette, she wrote – or the spirits wrote – at least 10 times as fast as normally. Also, the handwriting itself was entirely different for Mother always wrote in a small cramped hand, except when using the planchette. Mother's mediumship remained with her until she joined Father in her 83rd year.

As we went from the 1880s into the Gay 1890s the weekly seances took on a somber tone. Warnings were given constantly that some sort of disaster was going to strike our country. It seemed the spirit controls could not tell us the exact sort of disaster that was soon to come upon us. Father was urged to liquidate much of his income property but failed to do so. The disaster came in the form of the Panic of 1893. Our family lost most of everything we possessed. Still we were better off than many others who were reduced to absolute poverty.

Father had been told not to trade his business building at on Kansas Avenue. The spirit voice warned that if he did he would sustain quite a loss. He traded. He lost. He was told that he would remove his family from Topeka to Kansas City and, although at the time he had no such idea, we did move to Kansas City where he passed on in 1920.

In our seance group there was no reason for trickery or fraud and there was none.

I have attended home seances in many lands and my assurance that man cannot die has been reinforced through the years.

I wish to repeat my former statement: if you are searching earnestly, honestly, sincerely for the proof that man cannot die you can discover this truth in your own home seances.

FATE 1958

# SUICIDE FROM THE OTHER SIDE
## Susan Rushing

If you take your own life, you are condemned to the eternal fires of hell. That is that. At least that is what I was told by my parents, my church and even an assembly I once attended in junior high school. I remember that assembly as if it happened only yesterday. I was 13 or so, sitting in a dark auditorium, listening to a teenaged boy on a recording. He was sad, at his wit's end, apologizing for the failure that he had been to his friends and parents. At the end of his speech there was a long pause and then a loud bang. It startled us all, and somebody even screamed.

Then the lights came up and one of the presenters stood in a single spotlight and said, "That poor boy is now burning forever in hell. That is what happens when you decide to take your own life. You burn in hell."

I still remember the horror I felt and the scenario that played in my mind of him lying in his room and then onto the hysteria of his parents finding him.

So, they made their point. I remember thinking, even at that age, what a disappointment that God would not take mercy on that sad young man. I bought what they sold, but deep down inside it didn't feel right.

## The gift of sight

Thirty years later I would realize that, without a doubt in my mind, it wasn't right.

Sometimes gifts come to us in unusual ways. This particular gift came to me in the form of a request for a free reading from an event promoter. The promoter told me that she had a friend who was in a bad place in her life and she felt that I was the one who could help her out. I agreed to the reading, and in my self-centered fear, I felt taken advantage of. Little did I know this reading would turn out to be a bigger gift to me than my small-mindedness could have ever imagined at that moment.

I had assumed that this would be another reading of dire questions about some cheating man or quests for predictions of real estate transactions. Imagine my shock when, on the other end of the phone line, was a sobbing woman whose son had committed suicide just three months before. My head began to spin as I prayed to be given the best information possible for this woman. All the while she was crying and begging me to try to connect with her son. I prayed, "Jesus, if you have ever given me the good stuff, it has to be now. I can't hurt this woman any more than she already hurts."

Without a moment passing, into my vision came a young man with shaggy brown hair. Amazingly, he was being brought forward, almost carried under the arms by two massive angels. I could not believe what I was being shown.

They took him close to me. He looked exhausted, his head hanging down with dark circles under his eyes. He gave me messages for his mother of apology. He had been sick in thought; his mind swirling and swirling for years. He had been addicted to drugs and had recently gotten clean. But being clean made his thoughts begin to swirl again and he said that he just couldn't take it any longer. He told me that he was okay. He also explained that he had work to do and that if his mother needed him, to just ask. His energy was low, but he explained that he could be in several places at a time.

I communicated for over an hour, my mind trying to process all this new and confusing information and give messages to his mother at the same time.

When we ended the reading, the mother seemed to feel better about where her son was and how he was doing. I, on the other hand, had some serious questions that would not leave. After all, I believed that once you crossed to the other side it was all love and forgiveness, peace and tranquility. Were there really the harsh punishments and judgments that I had been warned about in my youth? The young man, however, was tired, exhausted. He didn't seem happy or rejuvenated or any of the things that I had imagined would happen when a soul crossed over to the other side. It was perplexing. Not wanting to question what Spirit gives me during my readings, I set it aside in my mind for the rest of the night and well into the next day.

## Searching for answers

When I finally went into meditation, late the next day, I asked for any messages from my guides and angels. I received a small, almost greeting-card-like message. Definitely not a typical message from my usual long-talking guides. I closed my eyes again and focused in and asked why my message was so short. The response I received was, "It is not the answer you truly seek."

As usual, they were right. It wasn't what was on my mind. I wasn't really sure I wanted to know the answer to the question. That was pretty deep stuff, and I wasn't sure I was ready. Then I realized that if I hadn't been ready, my guides would not have been so eager to share the information. So, I took a deep breath and asked, "What were those angels?"

The message I was given was this:

"You are correct in that they are guardians or sentries. They are charged with guarding the souls that come to them for healing. You are incorrect in your thinking of this soul's captivity. This is a situation of protection of the soul.

"There is accountability, but not as you have imagined. Each one must be responsible for the seeing, the feeling and the aiding in the repair of the deficit of energy that they have left in ending their life. They must see the grief that they have caused. They must feel the grief that their loved ones are feeling. As situations arise, it is in their power to be of assistance; they must aid to repair the situation as it is brought before them. It is this accountability. It is all in the realm that you call Heaven. They are in the care and the love of the Father for all time."

The angels had to bring this young man forward during the reading to help him repair some of the deficits that he had left for his mother. They accompanied him because his energy was not strong enough for him to come through on his own, and it was not strong enough to get him back to the other side without assistance.

I was shown a place that suicide victims go to once they cross. It made me think of a hospital. My guides helped me understand that the majority of people who take their life are spiritually ill. They have lost hope and light and are in need of a great deal of love. Special angels were here to surround them with love and healing. They could stay as long as they needed, before continuing their soul's journey in another realm. Some souls stay longer and participate in the healing of others. Some stay for a very long time. There seemed to be no timetable. It was very quiet and peaceful with soft pink love energy everywhere.

It became clear to me that suicide does not condemn a soul to hell, but neither is it an easy way out.

The work that waits on the other side is clearly supported in love, but it seems a long, sad and tiring journey to fix something that should not have been broken. I am hoping as I write this that the young man that came through in my reading is healing well and finding some peace. I pray for the family that he left behind and hope that they are doing the same.

*Susan Rushing: Generational psychic/medium.*

FATE May-June 2011

# THE SECRET OF INSPIRATION STUMP
## Marcia Masino

There are mystical places in the world where we can effortlessly hear the whispers of spirits, and sometimes they actually transfigure their images onto us. "Inspiration Stump," an actual tree stump situated in a clearing of the magnificent Leolyn Woods of Lily Dale, New York, is one of those rare settings where spirits draw close.

Lily Dale is the largest Spiritualist Church Assembly in the world. The community was founded in 1879 as a summer camp retreat for Spiritualists near beautiful Cassadaga Lake. Located in southwestern New York State, Lily Dale has been dedicated to the preservation and promotion of the religion of Spiritualism for 125 years. It still thrives today with homes, places of communion with spirits, a post office, an auditorium, a healing temple, stores, a library and the Museum of Spiritualism.

Visitors from all over the world flock to Lily Dale every summer seeking peace, tranquility, metaphysical education and messages from departed loved ones through the mediums who reside there. Spiritualists believe in the continuity of life after the transition called death, and that this is proven by the communication with the spirit world provided by a medium.

## Inspiration Stump

Within the Lily Dale community is the Leolyn Woods, where the Inspiration Stump is situated in a clearing surrounded by ancient trees. The Native Americans regarded the Stump as a special healing tree. Eager souvenir hunters damaged the tree over time, and so a cement replica was created over the original stump. During July and August, the woodland clearing has park benches for services where mediums serve as messengers for spirit communication.

As a teacher of psychic phenomena, I want my students to have a firsthand experience of the spectral realm. I teach them about the psychic gifts of clairvoyance or psychic vision; clairaudience, the hearing of intuitive messages; and clairsentience, the sensing and knowing of psychic information. These intuitive faculties are used by the medium to contact and channel spirits and spiritual energy. Mediumship is defined as the ability to communicate with the spirit world, bringing helpful and inspirational messages from loved ones to a person on the Earth plane. Lily Dale has a beautiful, peaceful essence; there is no better place to take individuals in search of a positive mystical experience.

The nighttime path to the Stump is dark. Fireflies twinkle inside the woods, and it seems as if the stars have fallen from the sky. My students use the crunch of gravel and the flickering light of the fireflies to find their way, and they wonder if they have stumbled into a different reality, as if they were in Shakespeare's play *A Midsummer Night's Dream*.

## Spirits all around

You may see spirits seated alongside you or sense them standing in the area. I often sense Lily Dale's forefathers seated on the benches. It seems that a natural setting of ancient growth forest is also inspirational to the spirits. People have seen fairies dancing around the Stump area as well as ethereal animals that appear as totems of protection for them.

One of my favorite experiences is taking students to the Stump for the first time. As their eyes adjust to the darkness of the woods lit eerily by the rising moon, they often see an imposing figure walking around the Stump area. "It looks like a Native American Indian Chief," they excitedly exclaim. Known as "The Guardian of the Stump," this Indian spirit has been seen standing guard for decades by mediums. Entities can adopt a location, developing a loving custodial relationship with it, and dedicating themselves toward keeping its energy sacred.

*Inspiration Stump at Lily Dale Assembly.*

## Site of transfiguration

For those seeking a firsthand mystical contact, Inspiration Stump at night offers a glimpse into the rare phenomenon of transfiguration. This occurs when a spirit superimposes onto you, transforming your appearance in order to communicate a message. My students take turns standing before the group. I can see the faces of their ancestors superimposed upon them and am able to provide a detailed description of them.

Beth appeared as her usual self at first, but then I saw a different face transfigure over hers, complete with an old-fashioned bonnet and an actual change in stature. Beth seemed to grow smaller. She confirmed that, historically, her family members were small in stature and were pioneer settlers, explaining the bonnet on her head.

Once the flow of images began they changed rapidly, and I then witnessed Beth's spirit guide. She changed completely into a woman of Polynesian appearance, resplendent with long, flowing black hair. Her form was wrapped in a softly shimmering sarong, bathed in the glow of the moonlight. The spirit guide smiled knowingly, and I sensed that her name was Oceana. As I spoke her name aloud, Beth's eyes, hands and ears began to glow in a vibrant blue color. I instantly knew that Oceana was revealing Beth's psychic gifts. She could see, sense and hear spiritual energy. Oceana was her spirit guide, serving as both teacher and protector for her journey of psychic development. As I finished describing what I had just seen, she faded away. A brilliant yellow light in the shape of an infinity symbol glowed from Beth's forehead area. I knew that the transfiguration experience had created an initiation for Beth, introducing her to her spirit guide.

## Dispersing dark energy

Olivia stood near the Stump while Jennifer watched a cluster of dark energy appear at the base of her spine. It looked to Jennifer as if a black knife were lodged there. She described it to Olivia so that she could focus on the area too. "It feels like there is no energy moving there, like it is blocked," Olivia commented. She then asked Jennifer to help her send healing energy to that area to disperse the negativity that had gathered there. After a few minutes, Olivia felt a shift, a release. The energy block had dispersed. For the first time in a long while, Olivia slept well that night. Her confusion about her life purpose seemed to have disappeared. After her experience at Inspiration Stump she began to acknowledge her deep-seated desire to become a healer. The Stump's special spiritual energy had started the transformation of Olivia's life.

Darius felt completely out of place as he sat with the group in the dark. Suddenly he felt the back of his head nudged and turned around to see who was playing games with him. "I could've sworn I felt the back of my head swatted!" he exclaimed. I asked him who that action reminded him of. He thought for a moment, then remembered that his deceased grandfather had the habit of playfully hitting the back of his head. He then revealed that he'd dreamed of his grandfather that morning. Grandfather was using the Stump opportunity to let Darius know he was still around and watching over him. "Yeah, maybe," he responded unenthusiastically. Just then he felt a physical push from behind and lunged forward; he was being told to listen.

## The Easter Bunny

Spirits aren't always serious; sometimes they use a lighthearted approach to get their message across. Lynn stood in front of the Stump while the rest of the students peered into the darkness. Suddenly John saw a brilliant green light swirling about her. Then John saw Lynn dressed as the Easter Bunny; she was holding an Easter basket and gathering various colored eggs to put into it. He felt that the message to her was that she was so busy "gathering eggs" that she wasn't paying attention to what she already had; the answers she sought were already in her basket. Lynn felt that the re-direction toward appreciation of who she already was and what she had accomplished was indeed helpful, since she was too focused on gathering more and more experiences and information rather than acknowledging what she had already accomplished and knew.

Brian's experience at the Stump was particularly poignant. As he stood before the group, one student, Erica, saw him transfigure into a World War II pilot. As she spoke of this to Brian, he spontaneously burst into tears. "I've dreamt of this man and the experience of dying as a war pilot for years and never told anyone."

For Erica, this was an important validation and verification of her budding mediumistic talents. For Brian, it was much more. "Every Veteran's Day I am overwhelmed with patriotism and feel choked up with pride and grief. This must be how soldiers feel. I never had an explanation for this gut reaction I've had for years," he said with relief.

Sometimes spirits choose to hang around us to experience what they missed in life, like an unseen friend. The mystical experience of transfiguration had resolved an unasked question that had weighed heavily upon Brian.

The Inspiration Stump area has always felt to me as a portal into another, higher dimension. The veil between this world and the next is very thin there. Psychic phenomena of a mystical nature have a peaceful, healing quality that is the true essence of Spiritualist communication.

## Transformation at the Stump

The transfiguration experiences at Inspiration Stump changed my students. Beth's introduction to her spirit guide, Olivia's decision to become a healer, Lynn's Easter basket message and Brian's revelation all fostered a closer relationship with each of their spiritual natures. Once this happens great transformations can occur. They were given the gift of peace of mind and soul guidance through their connection with the spirit world. My students had opened themselves to the experience of receiving spiritual messages and had come to truly understand why this special setting is called Inspiration Stump.

*Marcia Masino: Astrologer, author and Tarot reader.*

FATE July 2004

# HOW TO TALK TO THE DEAD
## Corrine Kenner

Soon after Sarah's 24-year-old son, Andrew, was killed in a motorcycle accident, she and her family experienced a heartwarming reunion with his ghost.

"I was standing in our kitchen before Andrew's memorial service," the Colorado dental hygienist recalled. "Kyle, our other son, came over and put his arm around me. Then my husband, Doug, came over to us, and we opened into a three-way hug. As we stood there silently with tears rolling down, we felt a light pressure, a light caress on our shoulders. In my heart I knew it was Andrew – and Doug and Kyle did too. We all felt the warmth of his embrace and his love. And mentally I heard Andrew say, 'Hey, guys, it's okay.'

"This lasted no more than 30 seconds, and then the warmth and the pressure were gone. But Andrew's hug had made us a complete family one last time."

Though to some it sounds bizarre, people have communicated with spirits for thousands of years. In fact, Spiritualism became a worldwide phenomenon during the last century. Today, professional mediums like Suzane Northrop and James Van Praagh are booked years in advance. They and their clients report that communicating with the dead is truly a healing gift.

"Visionary encounters with loved ones are not frightening," writes Raymond Moody, MD, in his book *Reunions: Visionary Encounters with Departed Loved Ones.* "On the contrary, they tend to be positive experiences that give people hope and a sense that the departed is comfortable, happy and still with them spiritually."

Some contact, like Sarah's, seems to occur spontaneously. In fact, that's how many professional mediums first discover their gifts. Communication with the dead, however, can be consciously developed. The techniques are relatively simple. It just takes faith, preparation and practice.

"Communication can come in surprising ways," Richard Webster says in his book *Spirit Guides and Angel Guardians,* "but we must be prepared to listen."

## Who's there?

Edith, a Florida bereavement counselor, is well-acquainted with death. Even she was surprised, however, when she received a touching farewell from one of her patients, a 65-year-old man named Howard who had ALS (also known as Lou Gehrig's disease).

"I was at home," Edith told researchers Judy and Bill Guggenheim, "when the nurse from hospice called to tell me Howard was actively dying – a process that can go on for hours. His wife was having a real difficult time and wanted me to come over and be there with her.

"I said, 'Of course' and went to change my clothes.

"I was in my walk-in closet, when all of a sudden I experienced Howard's presence. He was there on my right side. There was a lightness of being – a joy and a sense of freedom. It was like I heard in my heart his good-bye and a thank you for being there for him as I had been. He wasn't there long, probably about 30 seconds.

"When I stepped out of the closet, I looked at our digital clock, which said 4:23. I proceeded to get dressed and drove to Howard's house. When I walked in, they told me he had passed on at 4:23."

Howard's message was not unusual. Experts like the Guggenheims, who published hundreds of similar accounts in *Hello from Heaven,* say the dead frequently bring messages of hope and light to those they have left behind.

James Van Praagh has been a professional medium for many years, and he is the author of the best-selling book *Talking to Heaven.* "As a medium, I have never experienced anything but love and compassion and healing in my work,' he said. "It is the love bond between people which allows me to make the connection between the living and the dead."

Suzane Northrop, author of *The Séance,* concurs. "Their primary desire is simply to let you know that they are fine, not dead, and that they will be with you when it's your time," she said. "They don't usually need to do or say more, although you may want more."

## Isn't it dangerous?
It's natural to feel a certain reluctance to talk to the dead. The topic is surrounded by mystery, social taboo, and, for many, a sense of danger.

"Unfortunately, some people react with fear when they have an after-death communication," the Guggenheims say.

This is usually because they are startled by the suddenness of the event, or they may have never heard of one happening to anybody else. Such people may assume they are losing their mind. And others find it difficult to reconcile after-death communications with their philosophical or religious beliefs."

Professional mediums and parapsychologists offer reassurance and encouragement.

"God has granted you natural protection by allowing only those you permit to contact you, through your thoughts or mind," Northrop says. "I believe that this is one reason that contact for most people is so difficult, that this is God's way of protecting you from any contact outside of the light or contacts attempted without permission. What seems an obstruction is in fact a protection."

Raymond Moody, who also wrote the groundbreaking book *Life After Life,* consulted other experts about possible danger.

"Dr. William Roll, one of the world's leading experts on apparitions of the deceased, informed me that he had never once uncovered a case in which harm had come to anyone from an apparition.

In fact, unlike the popular image portrayed in horror films and books, he found these experiences to be beneficial in that they alleviate grief or even bring about its resolution."

## Religious restrictions

Moody says that many people grow up believing that attempting to talk to the dead violates religious tenets.

"Religious establishments depend heavily for their continuance on instilling rigid ideological beliefs about body, mind and spirit in their members," he says. "This includes discouraging them from seeking spiritual experiences on their own. After all, a psychological pioneer in the congregation who explores hidden realms of the self may well make discoveries that are difficult to reconcile with official doctrines.

"As for the intimations of some in the religious community that the forces of evil are itching to corrupt us... I suspect they are attempts to scare us into ideological conformity."

Such doctrine, however, may be less rigid than many believe. John Hooper, a writer for the *London Observer Service,* made waves when he reported that communication with the dead doesn't necessarily contradict Catholic teachings.

"One of the most authoritative spokesmen of the Roman Catholic Church has raised eyebrows among the faithful by declaring that the Church believes in the feasibility of communication with the dead," Hooper wrote. "The Rev. Gino Concetti, chief theological commentator for the Vatican newspaper, *L'Osservatore Romano,* denied he was signaling any change in approach. But he agreed that his remarks might come as a jolt to many believers.

"He said the Church remained opposed to the raising of spirits, but he added: 'Communication is possible between those who live on this Earth and those who live in a state of eternal repose, in heaven or purgatory. It may even be that God lets our loved ones send us messages to guide us at certain moments in our life.'

"Concetti suggested dead relatives could be responsible for prompting impulses and triggering inspiration – and even for 'sensory manifestations' such as appearances in dreams.

"Concetti said the new Catholic catechism specifically endorsed the view that the dead could intercede on Earth, and he quotes the dying

St. Dominic telling his brothers: 'Do not weep, for I shall be more useful to you after my death and I shall help you then more effectively than during my life.'"

## Spontaneous communication

Though Northrop stresses that not every dream involving a dead relative is an attempt at contact, for most people, visits from their late loved ones usually do occur in dreams.

"Why? Because information from the spirit world or dead people comes through our right brain," she says. "For this to happen easily, the analytical side needs to abstain or be pushed into the background."

Of course, there are other means of contact, such as the phantom phone call described on March 3, 1998, by *Miami Sun-Sentinel* writer Donna Pazdera.

"The woman who called Jerrod Zelanka's house early Sunday was crying and her voice was faint," Pazdera wrote.

"I'm at the bottom of a dark hole," the woman said. Then the line went to static. Zelanka hit *69, a code used to trace the call, but the number could not be pinpointed.

"Now, Zelanka and others think that call somehow was made by his friend, Leah Jean Ash, 20, after she and a friend had an accident on an all-terrain vehicle late Saturday. Both were found dead early Sunday on the bank of a drainage canal after an accident.

"'The strange part is, neither carried a cellular phone that night, Parkland Police Chief Steve List said.'"

## Summoning spirits

If talking to the dead is possible – and, in fact, even natural – experts say we can actively pursue such contact.

"Everyone can develop intuition," Van Praagh says. "Once you realize there is no death, that life goes on, there's no reason to have fear."

The procedure can be as simple or as elaborate as you like. Experts recommend a number of techniques.

Their first suggestion? Meditate.

"Meditation will enable you to relax and soften any fear or anger you may have," the Guggenheims say. They recommend it for people who have unresolved emotions surrounding the death of a loved one."[Meditation] will also allow you to unfold your inner, intuitive senses," they say. "In fact, you may have an after-death communication experience while you are meditating. Ask for a sign that your relative or friend continues to exist. Pray for him or her and others who are affected by the death, including yourself."

Other suggestions include:

1. Set an appointment. Be specific. Repeat silently or aloud: "Monday, at seven o'clock for the next month, I'll be open to receiving communication from ... "

2. Starting the day before you attempt to communicate with the dead, forgo caffeinated beverages, which can interfere with your receptive ability.

3. Other experts, including Moody, also suggest that you eat lightly, to further attune yourself to the spirit world. Try sticking to fruit and vegetables and skip dairy products.

4. Before you begin any session, take a walk outside to boost your connection to the natural world. Or, if you prefer, stroll through an art gallery or browse through a fine art book. Moody's studies found that such works also enhance spiritual contact.

5. Take some time to browse through photos and mementos of your loved one. Share their stories with other people and remember your favorite times together.

6. Find a comfortable place to sit in a private spot. Some people have good results outdoors, in a secluded, natural setting. Others are most at ease in a bedroom or den. Put up a "Do not disturb" sign if necessary.

7. A darkened room, lit only by candles, is a soothing aid to meditation and reflection.

8. Take off your watch, and make sure clocks are out of sight and out of mind. A sense of timelessness will help you connect to other realms.

9. Relax. "Properly relaxed, your arms will feel heavy and the tips of your fingers will tingle as though charged slightly by electricity," Moody says.

10. As you begin, picture yourself surrounded by white light. Silently or aloud, say, "Only with God's grace and allowance, those loved ones may come through." Northrop also recommends the Lord's Prayer or the 23rd Psalm. If your spirituality lies in other directions, pray or meditate in a way that is meaningful for you.

11. Enter the session in the spirit of fun. Just as you enjoy getting together with loved ones who are still living, you should look forward to encounters with those in spirit. Recall the pleasant times you shared. "Humor is the gateway to the paranormal for some people," Moody says.

12. And finally, don't try too hard. If nothing seems to happen, grant yourself permission to give up, and just enjoy a moment or two of relaxation. For many, that's when communication actually begins.

## What to expect

A shift in consciousness is usually the key to spirit contact. Some people report a tingling sensation. Others report a subtle change in their perception of their surroundings.

Northrop suggests that encounters with dead people will differ significantly from our interactions with the living. "You'll need to remember that communication with a person in spirit is different in method and components," she says.

Dead people communicate most frequently via audio signals and guided images, for example.

"The brain acts like a miniature radio tuning in to different frequencies and vibrations," she says. "We want to tune in to the frequencies where the dead folks are. You and the dead people are on different frequencies. You must raise your level of pitch and they must lower theirs in order for communication to take place. You will hear the message through your own mind. It will be their presence or words that are felt, but your mind is the receiver."

Richard Webster agrees. "Most people expect to see or hear their spirit guides using their eyes and ears. In fact, this is rarely the case. Our guides communicate to us telepathically and spiritually. We need to develop our spiritual vision in order to see them clearly. Often the message comes through as a faint, almost imperceptible intuition. Many times, a message from your guide will seem exactly like a thought and only later will you realize it came from your guide. If you are not open to receiving messages from your guides, they will remain unheard."

"The spirits communicate by their emotions," Van Praagh says. "No words exist in the English language, or any other for that matter, which can describe the intense sensations."

Don't be surprised if your visitor is someone other than the person you expected to see. That's not unusual.

In Moody's studies, "All of the subjects were prepared to see a specific person," he says. "Yet approximately one-fourth of the subjects saw a different deceased relative."

Once you make contact, don't try to push the encounter in a given direction.

"As a rule, I feel that you should not direct the experience at first," Moody says. "Instead, just let the images flow."

## Better late than never

The personality of those who have passed on is usually just as we remember. "If a person was talkative while alive, he will come through with plenty to say," Van Praagh says.

Those who recognize loved ones usually do so after a brief pause. "Apparitions of the deceased don't look exactly as they did before they died," Northrop says. "Strangely – or perhaps not so – they look younger and less stressed in their apparitional state, but still they are recognizable as who they are."

Molly, a stenographer in Missouri, told the Guggenheims how her 87-year-old grandmother appeared to her:

"My grandmother and I were extremely close. I lived a good part of my life with her. She was crippled from the time she was in her early twenties, so I never really saw her standing straight.

"The second night after her death, I was in bed but not asleep. My eyes were wide open, and I saw her! She was standing up straight and looked to be about 30 or 35 years old. She was solid and lifelike, just like a living human being.

"Her hair was cut short, and it was real curly all around her face. She had this sweet smile. She didn't say anything, but I got the idea that she was showing me, 'See, now I'm standing straight!'

"She was wearing an older style dress with an unusual pattern – a white background with a red stripe – that I didn't recall having seen. All she did was stand there and smile. I got out of bed and turned on the lights, but she was gone.

"I told my aunt about it the next morning. I described my grandmother's dress to her, and she took me to the basement and pulled out some old trunks. She found a quilt my grandmother had made. And there was the same material, that had a white background with a red stripe, sewn into the quilt!"

## Practice makes perfect

Once you've had some success in talking to the dead, keep it up.

"I had the gift as a kid," Northrop says. "But I did study. From day one I had teachers that were pretty strict. I've always taught that you can read a thousand books, but you really need to be with a professional who can help you fine-tune your gift."

Many professional psychics offer classes and workshops. Ask like-minded friends about their studies or seek recommendations and advice at New Age bookstores and shops.

For most people, contact with a deceased loved one is a sacred and profound experience to be cherished. Such communication usually expands one's understanding of life, can offer a deeper awareness of existence after death, and underscores an essential spiritual message: Life and love are eternal.

# Simple tools to strengthen your connection to the spirit world

Some people find that certain objects and rituals can help them make contact with their lost loved ones. Raymond Moody, MD, author of *Life After Life,* reported astounding success after he built a modern-day version of an ancient Greek psychomanteum in a converted Alabama mill.

He helped hundreds of volunteer test subjects see and talk to dead friends and relatives in a large gazing mirror. While the complete process is described in his book *Reunions: Visionary Encounters with Departed Loved Ones,* the premise is simple: Relax, reflect and gaze into any darkened reflective surface, such as a mirror; a crystal ball; polished metal; bowls or cup filled with water, ink, blood or wine; a polished lamp; a lake; even a window in a darkened room.

"At first," he wrote, "Some people report images that resemble the sky on a cloudy day. Others say that the mirror becomes darker. Whatever the case, this change in the clarity of the speculum signals that the visions are about to appear."

Soon after, test subjects described visions of their loved ones, and in most cases they could see and hear those spirits as clearly as they could when they were alive.

As with any psychic development activity, use these techniques only after you have calmed yourself – body, mind, and spirit – and pictured yourself bathed and protected in a field of white light. Doing so will help ensure that any messages you receive are pure and from their intended source.

**Photos and mementos:** These can bring the spirits of their former owners closer and are especially helpful as a meditation aid.

**Dream journals:** Because so much after-death communication occurs during dreams, keeping a record of contact can help you clarify messages and encourage repeat visits from the spirits of those you love.

**Seances:** Especially popular at the turn of the last century, seances with a group of trusted, like-minded friends are still an effective way of communicating with the dead.

**Ouija boards:** These are a simple way to connect with spirits, and often reveal clear, direct communication. Some psychic experts, however, advise using them with caution. "Mischievous spirits often appear when people play with devices such as the Ouija board without knowing much about them," says Richard Webster, author of *Spirit Guides and Angel Guardians.* "The Ouija board can be a useful instrument when used responsibly, but, unfortunately, it is promoted mainly as a parlor game, and it is not surprising that it attracts negative entities when used in this way. When you meet a new spirit, you should treat it with caution until you know exactly what it is. I am sure you do this when you meet new people. If you are in any doubt, ask the spirit whether it is of God, and see what response you get."

**Table tipping:** Start with just one other person, at a small, three- or four-legged table. Ask the table to tap once for "yes" and twice for "no." If you get good results, you might want to experiment with more complex codes.

**Pendulums:** Many people suspend a wedding ring from a piece of string or use a favorite locket. As with table-tipping, devise simple movements to respond to your questions.

**Automatic writing:** Sit in a comfortable chair, with a smooth, solid writing surface in front of you, a well-made pen in your non-dominant hand, and your arm bent at a 90-degree angle. You may notice your arm tingling before the automatic writing beings. Don't look or think too hard about what's being written. At first, you'll probably find just squiggles and circles. With time, however, you may discover that you have a gift for such correspondence.

## A firsthand account of a seance with Suzane Northrop

When Suzane Northrop appeared in Minneapolis recently, about 100 people paid $45 each for the chance to hear from those they'd loved and lost – and to learn how to talk to the dead themselves.

In the darkened sanctuary of a New Age church, with soft music playing, Northrop spent an entire Saturday afternoon sharing the gift she discovered in childhood. That's when her grandmother died of colon cancer. She says that as she stood by the casket, "My grandmother came and stood next to me. To me, she looked better dead than she had alive."

Northrop's grandmother even rode home with the family after the funeral, seated next to Suzane in the back seat, and shaking her head disapprovingly at her son's erratic driving.

Since that time, Northrop has been developing her talents for talking to the dead, writing and leading workshops around the country.

"Communication is easiest during the first three days after death," Northrop told the crowd. "It takes those three days for our outer energies to disconnect," she explained.

Contact continues during the course of the first year, and then tapers off. "Their job is to go on. Our job is to move on with our own life. When they come to us, they're in a much easier place. They come to whomever they possibly can to let them know they're all right."

After-death contact is important for both sides, she said. "It's not just about you. They benefit from it, too. They can get closure, and they can move on."

In a gray suit, with her shoulder-length brown hair parted in the middle, the New Yorker looked for all the world like someone you might see shopping in an upscale department store. But then she started pacing furiously in her ankle-high boots.

'I'm going to talk fast," Northrop said. "The information comes so quickly, it's hard for me to get it all across. But as long as you know what the dead people are talking about, that's all I care."

"Michael?" she called out to the audience. "Who here is connected to a Michael?"

One woman, weeping, raised her hand, and Northrop stopped mid-stride to talk to her.

"Your papa's gone, isn't he?" she asked. "And Michael hasn't let him go." Like most of the people Suzane would address that day, the woman nodded affirmatively.

Northrop moved on.

"There's somebody over here," she said, stepping a few feet away. "Walter. William. He's very pushy."

Another woman raised her hand.

"You were with him when he passed," Northrop said. Again, the woman nodded.

"He says he's still very handsome."

The woman laughed, and Northrop moved on, relaying greetings from the other side to almost everyone in the audience.

One woman's brother just wanted her to know that his hair is growing back. Another young man said he still likes motorbikes, even after death. Some of the dead people, Suzane said, were still wearing their favorite jewelry or hats. A few dead pets even showed up.

And in every case, Northrop said, the dead just wanted their loved ones to know that they had moved on, that they were doing well, and that they still watched over the living with fondness and affection, intervening whenever and however they could do so.

"They love to take credit for getting your mortgages through," Northrop told the crowd, "or getting you pregnant."

Northrop approached a woman named Carol, a realtor. "You lost a daughter?" she asked. The woman nodded. "You didn't lose a daughter," Northrop told her. "She hasn't gone anywhere. She's right here. She's with a dog and her grandma. And she talks. My God, does she talk. She still makes things with her hands; she wants you to know that. Is her father still here? He's a very lonely man. She says he blames himself. But your daughter is very happy that you've let her go."

Afterward, the woman confirmed that her daughter had been killed in her early 20s in a bicycling accident. All that Northrop had said was true.

"This is very intense subject matter," Northrop said later. "But I can reach people in a way I wouldn't otherwise. I can put it in a way that makes it seem safe. The bottom line is that death is a process that we're all going to go through. If we could live without the obsession that we die, I think we'd live our lives very differently. Where we might be limited, we become unlimited."

*Corrine Kenner: Writer and editor who specializes in astrology, Tarot and the paranormal.*

FATE August 1998

# TECHNOLOGY COMMUNICATION

# THE OTHER SIDE IS JUST A PHONE CALL AWAY
## Rosemary Ellen Guiley

It's a typical day in the New Reality world. You check your phone messages and find several from people who are living – and several from people who are dead. In your email box are similar messages from the living and dead, as well as emails from beings in other dimensions. And your computer has a new file of helpful information, materialized overnight by ethereal beings who are helping you with a project.

Sound far-fetched? Picking up your cell phone to call mom on the Other Side is not a reality yet, but research advances in technology for electronic voice phenomena (EVP) and instrumental transcommunication (ITC) are pointing in that direction. Science remains skeptical, but researchers all over the world who are dedicated to this work – as well as people who have had startling and comforting contacts – know that survival and communication between the living and the dead are real. What's more, bridges have been formed to other realms inhabited by higher spiritual beings – ethereals – and beings who identify themselves as extraterrestrials.

Researchers are improving their techniques and getting higher quality data. But ultimately the real success will depend not on machines, but on the consciousness of the people using the machines.

## EVP and ITC in a nutshell

EVP is the recording of voices for which there is no natural or scientific explanation. The voices usually are not audible during recording but are heard on playback; some devices for capturing EVPs enable real-time audible responses.

EVPs are controversial. Researchers believe they capture the voices of the dead, spirit beings and extraterrestrials, but skeptics contend the voices come from radio, television and citizen band (CB) radio transmissions, or are imagined from static and white noise sound. EVP voices often are faint and difficult to understand.

Mystery voices have been heard and recorded since the 19th century, manifesting in telegraph and telephone communications, radio broadcasts and phonograph and magnetic tape recordings.

Thomas Alva Edison believed that an electronic device could be built for communicating with the dead. He was fascinated by spirit photography and believed that if spirits could be captured on film, they could be reached electronically. Edison announced in the October 1920 issue of *Scientific American* that he was working on such a device. No one knows if he ever did, for nothing was completed – or even started – prior to his death in 1931. Nor did Edison, a prolific record keeper, leave behind any plans or notes for one.

In 1936, Attila von Szalay began experimenting with a record cutter and player to capture voice on phonograph records. He said that he began to hear a "tiny voice" in the air near him in 1938. He believed the voice belonged to his dead son, Edson. The experiments yielded what sounded like male and female voices, whistles and rapping sounds. In 1947, von Szalay tried using a wire recorder to improve his results but had difficulty with the wire.

In the 1950s, attempts were made by UFO enthusiast George William Hunt to tape paranormal and extraterrestrial voices. In 1956, von

Szalay and other researchers, including Raymond Bayliss and D. Scott Rogo, began experiments to capture voices on electromagnetic tape.

EVP remained in obscurity until an unexpected discovery was made by Friedrich Jurgenson, a Swedish opera singer, painter and film producer. In 1959, Jurgenson tape recorded bird songs in the countryside near his villa. On playback, he heard a male voice, speaking in Norwegian, discuss nocturnal bird songs.

At first Jurgenson thought it was interference from a radio broadcast, even though his villa was beyond the range of radio stations. He made other recordings to see if the same thing happened. Though he heard no voices during taping, many voices were heard on playback. Astonishingly, the voices gave personal information about him, plus instructions on how to record more voices.

Jurgenson wrote about his experiments in *Voices from the Universe,* published in 1964 with a record. In 1965, he met Konstantin

*Freidrich Jurgenson.*

151

Raudive, a Latvian psychologist and philosopher, who was so intrigued by the EVP that he devoted himself to researching it and recorded more than 100,000 voices over a period of years. Raudive published his research in German in *The Inaudible Made Audible,* translated into English in 1971 under the title *Breakthrough.*

*Konstantin Raudive.*

By the 1980s, thousands of EVP researchers around the world were recording messages from the dead and from more evolved spiritual beings who had once lived as humans on Earth. Many of the researchers were engineers and electronics experts who devised sophisticated experimental equipment setups for capturing the voices. Results varied by researcher, and the setups that worked for one often did not work for another, which complicated research efforts.

In 1982, Sarah Estep founded the American Association-Electronic Voice Phenomena in the United States, now run by Tom and Lisa Butler under a new name, Association TransCommunication.

The same year that the AA-EVP was founded, George Meek, a retired engineer, announced that he and a medium, William O'Neil, an electronics expert, had achieved success with an electronic device called Spiricom that could communicate with the dead. Meek, long interested in survival after death, had been given the idea for building a device by a discarnate scientist who communicated during a seance. The dead scientist told Meek he would cooperate in giving instructions.

Meek met O'Neil in 1977. O'Neil's spirit communicator delivered the technical information used by Meek and O'Neil to build Spiricom and said the device would make available thousands of sensitive frequencies that could reach into the Other Side.

Meek founded the MetaScience Foundation of North Carolina and invested more than half a million dollars of his own money in the research.

Spiricom allegedly enabled sustained, two-way conversations between the living and the dead, a vast improvement over the cryptic phrases characteristic of most EVP voices. O'Neil recorded some spectacular conversations he allegedly held with the dead.

Meek made available the plans for Spiricom devices to anyone at no cost. Unfortunately, no one who constructed the device reported success. EVP researchers theorized that Spiricom's success rested largely on the unique mediumship abilities of O'Neil. After the deaths of both O'Neil and Meek, evidence suggested that O'Neil – a ventriloquist – may have faked at least some of his recordings. The truth may never be known.

EVP has expanded into other media, including television, video and film cameras, and computers. As early as 1967, the deceased Edison purportedly came through a West German medium, Sigrun Seuterman, with advice for tuning television sets to 740 megahertz in order to receive paranormal effects.

In the 1970s, Viennese engineer Franz Seidl developed a way to get real-time voices by using a device that swept the radio band and created a jumbled noise background. Other researchers were finding that background noise, especially the so-called "white noise" of static, enhanced EVP.

ITC evolved from EVP, and includes unexplained phenomena involving all kinds of high technology in addition to voice recorders: television sets, computers, telephones, fax machines and so forth. Voices, photos, images, computer files and faxes are transdimensional communications, or "transcommunications," that is, sent from the higher realms to the physical. Those include the realm of the dead and other dimensions populated by higher beings. Some call these beings angels; in ITC they are referred to as "ethereal beings." They have no physical form and are more evolved than humans. Some experimenters receive contacts from higher beings, but the majority of EVP contacts are deceased humans.

In the 1980s, a Luxembourg couple, Maggy Harsch-Fischbach and Jules Harsch, inspired by the work of George Meek and William O'Neil, began experimenting with electromagnetic tape. They were contacted by ethereal beings who called themselves The Seven, part of a fraternity called the Rainbow People, who were interested in facilitating interdimensional communication. The Seven work in Time Stream, a collaboration of nonhuman beings and the human dead willing to work with the human living to form a bridge across realities. Key to the success of this communication, they said, is the consciousness and purity of motives of the living researchers. Greed, selfish intentions and desire for fame would doom any progress.

Jules and Maggy formed a group, the Cercle d'Etudes sure la Transcommunication (CETL), in 1985. After accomplishing major breakthroughs in TV, radio, computer and phone contacts, they joined with US researcher Mark Macy to forge the International Network for Instrumental Transcommunication (INIT) in 1995. The new field of ITC research spread around the world.

Almost as soon as it was formed, problems developed within the organization, however. Many researchers were not willing to share their trade secrets with others, and nearly all in the field feared being burned by derisive media attention. In addition, the lack of consistency in results achieved by certain setups of equipment posed a significant problem.

Why would one setup work for a researcher but not another? No one has the answer, but it probably lies in the realm of consciousness. Human consciousness "bonds" with devices, and the projections of consciousness affect results.

In 2001 INIT ended and Macy continued with his own organization, Worlitc.org, which he had founded in 1998.

Today, EVP has become a household term thanks to the media popularity of ghost-hunting shows and films, and to the persistence of researchers like Estep and the Butlers.

EVP and ITC have come a long way since the days of reel-to-reel and cassette tape recording. They comprise "etheric studies," according to Tom Butler, and involve mind-to-mind etheric connection between the human etheric self and nonphysical people and beings. The living are the mechanism by which the nonphysical can manifest in the physical world. The experimenter's intent is a major factor in results obtained. An open-minded, positive attitude encourages results.

Many of the high-level ITC contacts from other realms have dropped off since 2001, Macy said. Maintaining a rapport with the finer spiritual realms requires harmony and purity of intent among researchers, qualities that are difficult to sustain in human relationships. That became evident as squabbles led to a break-up of INIT. The ethereal beings who are participating in "the project" – building bridges between our world and finer spirituals realms – pulled back and are waiting for the right signals of consciousness. Macy is confident that humans will soon step up to the plate. "New frontiers of science will take us into the multi-dimensional," said Macy. "Soon we will have a new science based on spiritual principles in which time, space and gravity are reduced to illusory aspects of a more substantial reality of consciousness."

## Technology

How are EVP and ITC data transmitted? No one knows for certain, but communicators appear to modulate noise matrices provided by experimenters. For example, a video camera connected to a television set creates a feedback loop that produces a sort of visual static that otherworldly communicators can manipulate to form images. Similarly, a telephone hooked to a computer produces background noises that can be modulated into words.

Sonia Rinaldi, one of the leading researchers in Brazil, uses a video camera and computer in a mirrored hookup to create optical noise for the manifestation of images. Pictures also have appeared on televisions sets that are turned off.

Recordings of EVP have been made under Faraday room conditions, environments totally shielded from electromagnetic interference. The Faraday conditions rule out the possibility of picking up stray radio and cell phone signals, a favorite claim of skeptics. EVP also has been impressed on recording devices without the need of microphones. For example, Alexander MacRae, a Scottish engineer, has done ground-breaking work recording EVP on a device he invented: a biofeedback machine connected to a radio.

EVP and ITC have been analyzed with forensics software by Il Laboratorio in Italy, founded in 2001. According to Paolo Presi, who directs the laboratory, forensics voice analyses demonstrate that the sounds made by EVP voices are sometimes impossible to reproduce by the human vocal chords. Face recognition software has been used to correctly match ITC faces with photos of the deceased.

Some of the most unusual visual ITC work has been done by Alan and Diane Bennett, English mediums who participated in the famous Scole group mediumship experiments several years ago. The Bennetts photograph natural crystals at high magnification. Faces and images appear in the matrix of the crystals. Quartz yields the best results. The technique was inspired by a visionary dream in which an entity showed Alan a crystal.

## Real time phone calls and ET images

For more than a decade, Brazilian Sonia Rinaldi has used her own technique of a telephone connected to a computer to record real-time EVP phone calls between the living and the dead. This system enables her to have more control over how communications are recorded. A noise matrix is created by people enunciating the sounds of language read from a list. The communicators modulate words from those sounds.

"Even a cough or a door opening can be modulated," Rinaldi said. "But you have to offer them loud and clear voices if you want the same back." For attempts to contact specific deceased persons, Rinaldi uses gender and age appropriate readers. For communication with a dead child, a living child reads the phonetic sounds.

Results are immediate, she said, and sometimes the communicators start speaking before the experimenters, as though they know what is coming.

Rinaldi's system has been tested in Spain, Uruguay and Argentina as well as in Brazil. Since 1998, Rinaldi has recorded more than 350 phone calls, in which 160 involved parents who recognized the voices of their dead children. Her goal, she said, is to bring the dead into 3D image and voice.

Her EVP work led her into ITC, and work with a system involving a computer and video camera hooked together in a mirror mode. Real-time mirror images of living people are modulated by communicators to create new images.

Rinaldi said that around 2001, the communicators identified themselves as ETs; their presence had been around much longer. It was unsettling news, due largely to the negative portrayal of ETs in the media. "It was very difficult for me to think that I was in contact with ETs," Rinaldi said. "I was in a panic – in fact, I stopped recording for a month. I locked my lab and thought that I would never return to it. Then I received information that the entities had come to help, to better the contact with the earth. I decided to go on, and check and see if that was true. I became convinced, so now I try to help them. If they were not good, they could have destroyed my house, the city. They see a chance to help us."

The ETs requested the mirrored, split images of people. Where the images come together, they create one-half of their own image and the camera duplicates it. "It shows that the way they think is completely different from ours," Rinaldi said.

Sometimes Rinaldi holds a cloth over the person in front of the camera, and images appear on the cloth. They have created images of the dead and of themselves. They have big heads and animate their images in real time. Rinaldi said she had concluded that they are "advanced beings at a higher vibrational rate, with an advanced science."

## The quest for more data

The Association TransCommuncation wants to work with more scientists who are willing to examine the evidence for survival and communication. "We're trying to provide the scientific community with everything they need for input data," said Tom Butler. Needed are more trained experimenters, and a standardized system for cataloging transdimensional communication. Such a system would help to distinguish real experiences from more subjective or even imagined ones. For example, researchers acknowledge that many people interpret EVP transmissions by the heart as well as the head, especially when they are hoping for contact with dead loved ones.

Dr. Gary E. Schwartz, director of the VERITAS Research Program at the University of Arizona, devoted to survival of consciousness studies, expresses optimism that science will validate EVP and other survival research. "EVP is going to put the last nail in the coffin of the old paradigm of science," he said.

*Rosemary Ellen Guiley with a type of radio sweep ghost box called the "Minibox."*
*Credit: Adam Blai.*

## Paranormal investigation

The field of paranormal investigation – ghost hunting – has embraced EVP technology, favoring "real time" communication devices. Most of these devices, generically called "ghost boxes," employ radio sweep technology similar to that developed by Franz Seidl. Ghost boxes were "reinvented" for the paranormal field in the early 2000s. Some of the early boxes were called "Frank's Box" after Frank Sumption of Colorado. Sumption, a skeptic, originally built the devices to disprove contact with the dead and became a convert because of his results.

Ghost boxes can produce both real-time EVP as well as "passive" EVP, that is, voices not heard until playback. The use of radio sweep introduces the uncertain element of mistaking bits of broadcast for EVP. Nonetheless, many investigators have collected unexplained communications.

Other EVP technology popular in the paranormal field is the "ghost app," software developed for cellphones and laptops. They employ built-in random dictionaries, echo chambers and other features intended to facilitate EVP.

*Rosemary Ellen Guiley: Author, researcher and Executive Editor of* FATE.

FATE September 2006

# SPIRIT VOICES: WHISPERS FROM THE OTHER SIDE
## Harry Warren

Back in the early 1970s, I saw a television program about tape recordings of disembodied spirit voices. Inspired, a friend and I decided to experiment with two ordinary tape recorders. Much to our surprise, we recorded some short staccato sentences – voices that apparently came out of nowhere.

In the process, I learned that recording voices from the Other Side is a remarkably simple process that anyone can learn – and that the range of electronic voice phenomena (EVP) is broad and fascinating.

The program featured a number of researchers, among them Friedrich Jurgenson, whose recorded mystery voices in 1959 in Sweden while trying to capture bird songs. He felt that the voices were speaking personal messages to him and were not from Earth. After four years of experimental recording, Jurgenson called an international press conference to announce to the world what he had discovered, and his book *Roestema Fraen Rymden (Voices from the Universe)* appeared the following year in Stockholm.

Another researcher featured was Dr. Konstanin Raudive, a Latvian psychologist and philosopher, who became so prominent in the field that for a time, EVP voices were known as "Raudive voices."

On the program I saw that momentous evening, several researchers demonstrated their recordings of various electronic voice phenomena. All of them had simply addressed questions to the spirit world, asking if anyone from the "other side" would like to respond. They then switched on a tape recorder hoping to record voices from Beyond.

When they had played back the tapes, these researchers heard voices – from no apparent Earthly source. The researchers claimed that the voices were communications with the spirits of the dead.

The voices seemed to speak with an unearthly speed. Typically, they were staccato bursts of monotone speech, short words joined together with no breaks or pauses between words. It took some effort to decipher what was said. The voices conveyed personal information for the researchers themselves – as if the spirits were aware that they were being taped and they wanted to get a message through to their loved ones.

The television program suggested that with a little care and simple equipment viewers could conduct similar experiments. So, a friend and I decided to try it.

We were surprised at the ease with which we produced our first example of "Raudive voices." Oddly enough, my friend's sheepdog refused to remain in the room when we played the tape. Animals are more psychically aware than humans, and the dog vacated the room posthaste whenever the tape was played.

We decided to attempt a second recording with additional tape machines. We gathered some friends in the living room. We arranged five ordinary cassette tape machines around an octagonal Victorian table. Then we laid our microphones in a circle around the table. Some of the recorders had automatic recording level controls. The more expensive recorders could be adjusted.

It was a dark, fogbound night, partly illuminated by a full moon. When we were ready to begin we turned off the lights to add more atmosphere to the proceedings. The only light entering the room was from a street lamp outside.

We synchronized the start of the tape recordings by powering the recorders from a strip socket which had an electrical on/off switch.

We had a lighthearted, open-minded attitude, which is essential to any psychic contact. Some of us laughed nervously as we asked if there was anyone present from the spirit world who would care to leave a message on our tapes. Then we waited in total silence in the darkened room, watching the red glow from a sports timer as it counted the seconds. We switched off the recorders after precisely three minutes. With the lights back on, we eagerly rewound our cassettes to find out if we had recorded anything unusual.

We pressed the playback button on each tape recorder in turn and listened intently. First, we heard a few seconds of our own laughter, followed by a period of silence and tape hiss. There didn't seem to be any sign of voice phenomena – but then to our surprise, we heard something.

First came the sound of a creaking floorboard followed by heavy footsteps. The sound of the footsteps grew louder as they entered the room, then paused momentarily. Then they continued walking, until they gradually faded into the distance.

Each cassette had recorded the footsteps, but none of us in the room had heard any footsteps until we played back the cassettes. Suddenly we began to realize that what we had started in a semi-serious manner had become very serious indeed. I felt afraid. Whose footsteps were those? Where had they walked?

Our friend who lived in the house recognized the sound of the creaking floorboard immediately. He said a loose board at the entrance to the room always creaked when trod upon. Was this the starting point of the footsteps? To find out, we played the first recording while our friend walked in sequence with the sounds of the steps on the recording.

He walked in exact time with the recording, stepping into the room and following the sound around the table. When the footsteps on the tape paused momentarily, we all realized that whatever had made the footsteps had stopped exactly where our friend had been sitting. The color drained from his face. As the footsteps resumed, our friend continued around the room, until he reached the door again and the sound faded away.

We were astonished. None of us had expected such an outcome to our experiment. Raudive recordings are usually indistinct sounds that require careful interpretation. These were clear, audible recordings of footsteps!

Our friend was especially frightened. He invited his mother to listen to the tapes. She thought we had been play-acting at first, but as she listened she became sure that the recordings sounded like the footsteps of her late father. He had been a fit old gentleman until he died in his late eighties. He had usually worn old-fashioned, heavy boots that resounded on the plain wooden floorboards. Each day after his morning stroll, he enjoyed reading the newspaper on his favorite easy chair – in the same living room where we had made the recordings.

The grandfather's one wish was for a grandchild, but he had died before our friend was born.

My friend's younger sister overheard our discussion and quickly grew frightened and upset. Our friend's mother forcefully told us to erase the recordings in her presence, chastised us for upsetting everyone, and sent us all home. She said we had become involved with something dangerous. (Later the family had a Mass said in the house on the anniversary of the grandfather's death, and no other phenomena occurred there.)

When our group of friends got together again, we discussed our results and decided that we had touched upon the supernatural. With the fright we had received we decided against any further experimentation. Had we invited a guest from the afterlife into our world?

I myself would like to believe it was the loving grandfather taking the chance to visit his grandson, using to his advantage a channel to the afterlife we had opened up however inadvertently. In some of us this experience set off a desire to know and understand the paranormal, and years later I began experimenting again with Raudive recordings.

## Spirit technology

I am analyzing the wave form pattern generated by spirit recordings. The computer program I am developing will allow a rough comparison with human voices. I hope to build a database of spirit voice patterns to establish how they differ from real human voices or electronically produced synthesized voices. If spirit recordings show a demonstrable difference from normal recordings, I hope to build a device specifically tuned and calibrated to aid in their recording and playback.

An unusual feature of spirit recording is that nothing strange is heard while one is taping; the voices only appear when the recording is played back. It is as if the spirit voices have to be electronically imprinted onto the tape, making real-time monitoring impossible. I propose to design and build a device for my computer that would allow me, while recording is taking place, to pass the signals through a computer buffer. This would allow me to set a programmable time delay so I could visually and aurally monitor a spirit recording session in almost real time on a computer screen just after the recording is imprinted on the tape.

## Try it yourself

It's not necessary to have computer equipment, however, to experiment with spirit voice recording. The simplest apparatus is a cassette recorder with a counter. That way you can rewind the tape to an exact location in your recording. Do not be afraid of attempting a tape recording if your recorder is old or very basic. The first and very fruitful recordings from the Other Side were made with the most basic of low-tech recording equipment.

Find a quiet spot and physically and mentally relax. Seat yourself comfortably and still your mind with meditation or a silent prayer. Politely and with an open mind ask if anyone from the spirit world would like to make contact. Then start recording on an unused tape for no longer than three minutes.

Rewind and play back the tape. Listen intently through the unavoidable tape hiss for the sound of voices. Use headphones to achieve the best results. Just above the background noise of the tape you may catch a word or phrase. With any luck you will be pleasantly surprised!

## The history of spirit contact

Humankind has long attempted spirit contact with physical aids, be it with crystal balls or high-tech equipment. As modern technology has advanced, so have the efforts at spirit communication.

In 1936 Attila von Szalay tried to capture paranormal voices on phonograph records with a Pack-Bell record-cutter. In 1947 he bought a Sears-Roebuck wire recorder and got better quality voices, but he had technical problems with the wire.

In 1971 English publisher Colin Smythe, Ltd. introduced an expanded English translation of Raudive's book *Breakthrough, an Amazing Experiment in Electronic Communication with the Dead.* Marcello Bacci and colleagues in Grosseto, Italy, made weekly contact with "spirit" communicators with a vacuum tube radio tuned to static, experiments which continued into the late 1980s.

In West Germany from 1982 to 1988, H. Otto Koenig developed sophisticated electronic equipment, using extremely low-beat frequency oscillators and ultraviolet and infrared lights, for spirit communication. From 1985 to 1988, Luxembourg's Jules Harsch and Maggie Harsh-Fischbach developed and operated two electronic systems superior to any of the EVP equipment in use up to that time, making spirit communication more dependable and repeatable on a limited basis.

Researchers in several countries have reported seeing pictures of the dead appear sporadically on television sets. Many ordinary people also have seen spontaneous images of departed loved ones on their televisions. The late Klaus Schreiber in Germany, with technical assistance from Martin Wenzel, developed equipment to get better control of these images of the dead, using opto-electronic feedback systems. Schreiber was able to get audio-video contact with his two deceased wives. Since his death, Klaus himself has appeared on researchers' televisions.

The most exciting and potentially fruitful development is computer communication. England's Kenneth Webster reportedly has received 250 communications from Thomas Harden, who lived in Webster's house during the 16th century. From the spirit world, Harden explained that he could see Webster's electronic equipment in the living room. Harden described Webster's computer as "a box with a multitude of lights, sitting near my chimney."

Harden would communicate in old English grammar in a variety of ways, including computer files written on the display screen and generated onto the computer's hard disk. Harden later was reported to have explained to Webster that the writing was formed according to his will or his visualization in the "lightbox." Webster wrote a book about his experience, *The Vertical Plane,* with extensive photo documentation.

*[Editor's note: Magnetic tape recorders have given way to digital recorders, laptops and smart phones, but some researchers still prefer magnetic tape, saying they achieve better results.]*

*Harry Warren: Techcommunications engineer and an amateur astronomer who lives in Ireland.*

FATE August 1997

# DEATH NO MORE A CASKET: THE EVP REVELATIONS OF SARAH W. ESTEP
## Rosemary Ellen Guiley

Sarah W. Estep was five years old when she saw her first dead person. The corpse in the casket convinced her that death is the end, a finality – there is no survival into an afterlife. Many years later, Estep had another profound experience: the voice of a dead person speaking to her on an audio tape. That experience propelled her into the exotic world of EVP – Electronic Voice Phenomena, the recording of voices of the dead, angels, ETS and other entities.

Today Estep is recognized as one of the world's leading EVP experts. She has collected thousands of EVP recordings, and she founded the American Association-Electronic Voice Phenomena, an organization she led for 18 years. In addition, Estep has had ET contact experiences and past life recollections, even photographing an ancient tomb in Egypt where she believes she was buried in a previous life. She has definite views on the afterlife. For someone who started life with the certainty that death is the end, she has had a long, mysterious and rewarding journey.

Thanks to the work of Estep and many others in the field, EVP has virtually exploded in popularity in recent years.

I was delighted to discover that Estep lives in Annapolis, Maryland, minutes away from my own home. She is a gracious and interesting person to visit, sharing her knowledge and experiences about communicating with the dead and other realms. I even got to try out taping for EVP on her equipment – with successful results.

## Is death really final?

Estep remembers well her pivotal point at age five, when she looked down at a corpse awaiting burial. Estep and her family lived in Altoona, Pennsylvania. Once a year they would visit her father's parents in Westfield, New York, who owned a funeral home. The family lived upstairs on the second floor, where Estep and her parents stayed. Five-year-old Estep was taken into a room where bodies were prepared for burial. There she saw a man laid out in a casket. Fascinated, Estep would sneak into the room to peek into other caskets.

"I'd slip in and very quietly close the door behind me," she recalled. "I'd walk over to the casket and I'd stand on my toes and put my hands on the edge and look down into the face of a dead person. I'd just stand there and look at them. I wasn't at all frightened. They were dead and I knew they couldn't hurt me. But I became convinced that once you die, you go into a hole in the ground. Death is a casket. I grew up thinking there was no life after death. There was no heaven, no anything. I didn't dare tell my parents or anyone. I didn't like that feeling, but I couldn't think anything else because I'd seen all these dead people."

Estep's turnaround came in 1976, when she read *The Handbook of Psi Discoveries* by Sheila Ostrander and Lynn Schroeder. There were two chapters on EVP that discussed the work of Konstantin Raudive, Friedrich Jurgenson, Harold Sherman and Walter and Mary Jo Uphoff. The evidence for survival challenged and intrigued Estep. She decided to try EVP herself, using a large reel-to-reel tape recorder belonging to her husband, Charlie. She committed herself to a week of trials. If she got no results during that time, she would abandon the effort.

Every morning, Estep went down into her basement and tried to capture voices on tape. She returned late at night to check for results. She asked one question over and over again: "Is anybody here?"

*Sarah W. Estep. Credit: R.E. Guiley.*

For five nights, nothing happened. "I was bored to death," Estep said. "I thought that if someone was listening on the other end, they must be as bored as me."

On the sixth morning, she changed her question to, "Please tell me what your world is like." A clear female voice replied, "Our world is one of beauty."

Thankful and delighted, Estep decided to continue her EVP experiments, only to be greeted by silence for nearly a month. Just as she was ready to quit again, she heard voices say, "Don't give up" and "Keep it up." After several months of more experimentation, Estep recorded voices nearly every time she tried.

Estep taped seven days a week and received three to four messages a day. She kept up her practice until 2000, when she cut back to occasional taping. Her vaults now contain 25,000 recordings, about 22,000 of which are dead human beings now living in the realm of spirit. About 2000 seem to be extraterrestrial, and the remaining 1000 are beings from other worlds or dimensions.

171

About 90 percent of all the voices sound male. "I'm not sure why that is," said Estep. "Perhaps it has to do with the technology of EVP."

The quality of the voices, and the ease with which they could be understood, varied significantly. Estep used and popularized the classification system established by Konstatin Raudive, and still used by researchers today:

- Class A voices are clear, can be heard without headphones and can be duplicated onto other tapes.
- Class B voices are less clear but may not require headphones to understand them.
- Class C voices are faint and fragmented. They usually require headphones but still may be indecipherable.

In 1982, Estep founded the American Association-Electronic Voice Phenomena, one of the largest nonprofit organizations devoted to the study of EVP. She directed it until 2000, when she turned it over to the leadership of Tom and Lisa Butler. It is now called Association TransCommunication.

In 1996, the Dr. A. Hedri Foundation for Exopsychology and Epipsychology awarded Estep and George Meek its prize for Epispsychology, in recognition of their accomplishments.

## Personal revelations

I asked Estep what she had learned from her years of EVP work. She said that she became convinced of survival after death within the first six months of EVP recording. "After death, I think we all go to a world that is waiting for us," she said. "Humans go to their own place, and other beings from other worlds go to their own places." As for reincarnation, we stick to our original kind. Humans reincarnate as humans, and so forth. I know I have lived in this world many, many times," said Estep.

Some of Estep's most profound past-life EVP experiences occurred during her three trips to Egypt, where she feels she had several past lives. She even found a desert cemetery where she believes she was buried more than 2000 years ago. She took a recorder into tombs and pyramids and captured voices. In an ancient cemetery, a female voice said, "I buried you." In a small pyramid she got a voice of a boy, perhaps about 12 years old, who said, "My mother." Inside the Great Pyramid in Cairo, she was called by name. Voices asked if she could be trusted, and other voices answered, "Yes, she is a good person."

About six years after her first EVP results, Estep received a comment from the dead on her long-ago experiences as a child, when she concluded that "death is a casket" and the end to everything. A clear class A voice told her, "Death no more a casket."

"So, they knew me from the time I was five or six," Estep said.

## ET messages

During the first year of Estep's EVP work, she received strange messages that, because of their content, did not seem to originate from the realm of the dead but from extraterrestrial sources. Estep suddenly had the feeling that a transmission could come through her television set instead of her tape recorder. A voice told her to tune her set to channel 47 at night. After several tries, letters appeared on her screen. Estep initially was unable to interpret the message, but three days later, letters appeared that spelled recognizable words. The first word was VENUS, which appeared many times. The word ARRIVED came six days later.

Two weeks later, the ETs brought pictures to the television screen with words underneath. One was a circle with lines in it and the word VENUS beneath it. Next to it was a circle resting on a holder with the word WAR beneath it. Within 24 hours of this transmission, the United States took action to try to free American hostages held in Iran. Other pictures and words came through in the following weeks.

The ET voices talked about their own worlds. Their messages were longer than the short and clipped messages from the dead. Estep asked them about their god. They told her they have different gods. "Our god is with you," they told her, and she replied that she was honored that he came.

The television transmissions were accompanied by the manifestation of beings. Once Estep saw two beings who looked like human men, dressed in black uniforms, who were working on a small box in front of her television set. They said their craft was over her home or the river in front of it, and that they had brought down boxes to Estep's office. Estep had the impression that the boxes facilitated communication in English, and the appearance of images and symbols on her television screen. Her little French poodle, Misty, seemed to see the ETs and would shake all over when they appeared.

On another occasion, Estep asked ETs what color was their world. The answer was, "We look like yellow." Two nights later, Estep was visited by a bright yellow light the size of a basketball that came down from the sky and was visible through her home window. The next day she received the message, "We came down to see you."

In addition to Venus, ET messages have come from Mars and Alpha Centauri. Estep has received the most from Venus and has been told that Venus most closely approximates Earth in terms of life there.

Estep emphasizes that her relationship with the ETs who communicate with her is positive. "I have always felt close to them," she said. "They have never been terrible with me. I have had very good contacts with them." Some of her messages have been corroborated by messages received independently by other EVP researchers.

Estep has written two books, *Voices of Eternity* (1988) and *Roads to Eternity* (2004). *Roads to Eternity* is accompanied by a CD featuring spirit and ET voices from Estep's collection. Some of the voices are from scientists such as Charles Darwin and Arthur Stanley Eddington. The CD includes some of Estep's many contacts with Beethoven and features a musical chord and a minute of music from one of Beethoven's compositions, which is slightly changed from the original.

Estep's work has inspired many people to explore EVP and undertake research that someday may provide definite answers to the realms that lie beyond death, and to other places in the universe.

*[Sarah Estep made her transition to the Other Side on January 3, 2008.]*

*Rosemary Ellen Guiley: Author, researcher and Executive Editor of FATE.*

FATE December 2004

# TAPES FROM THE DEAD
## Sarah W. Estep

Since starting to record voices from other dimensions, my tape recorder and I have traveled more than halfway around the world together. At each stop I drift quietly off by myself and invite invisibles to speak through my small, battery-operated recorder. More often than not they reply.

I first read about EVP (electronic voice phenomena) in 1976. At the time I was a psychical investigator focusing on reincarnation and working mainly with children, but I was looking for something else. Being a pragmatic idealist, I was never sure if a particular case I was involved with was actual proof of reincarnation. There was evidence, at times a great deal, but evidence was not enough. I wanted more.

When I read about mysterious voices appearing on recording tape, I was skeptical. A person surely couldn't sit down at a tape recorder and ask the dead to speak and hope for any kind of an answer. I had always tried to be openminded as an investigator, and so I decided to try for seven days. If nothing was received by the end of that time I would forget the whole thing. Fortunately, on the morning of the sixth day, I

175

taped my first word, "beauty." Now, almost 14 years later, I'm still taping, and the invisibles are still talking. They have found a ready listener.

For many years it had been my hope to visit Egypt. Finally, in 1984, I made my first of three trips there. My tape recorder, a dozen 60-minute tapes, many batteries, and a battery checker were the most important part of my luggage. To insure safe arrival everything was hand carried, and the tapes and batteries placed in lead-lined bags so the x-ray equipment at the airport wouldn't affect them.

Up until my visit to the land of the Nile, I had occasionally taped outside of my home in a haunted location. I had discovered that voices were just as likely to speak to me in a haunted house 10 miles down the road as at home where I do most of my recordings – but would they continue to come through when I found myself in a strange, new world 6,000 miles away?

There were many questions in my mind that first morning when the bus picked up our group of 20 at the Mena House in Cairo. If anything came through my tape recorder, and I was not at all sure it would, would I be able to understand what they said? Perhaps it would be in Arabic, or an early Egyptian tongue that not even our guide would understand. Might I come in contact with some very "lost" souls who had been wandering around for 3,000 years, confused, frightened, perhaps bitter or even angry due to being in a condition they couldn't understand? If by some miracle they spoke, and spoke in English, would they make sense, or would it be the half-mad ravings of an emotionally disturbed ghost?

Some of my questions were answered that first morning. We were taken to Memphis, capital of the Old Kingdom of Lower Egypt. I felt self-conscious as I lowered my recorder into an open sarcophagus and asked if anyone had a message for me. After letting the tape run for about a minute, I ended the brief recording, as I ended all of the subsequent recordings during our tour with, "We leave you with love. We ask for your blessing." Since a taper doesn't know until he or she plays the recording back later whether a message has been received, I wondered if anything had come through.

As we were being driven to Sakkara from Memphis to see the famous Step Pyramid, I listened to the recording I had made an hour earlier. Within several seconds of my invitation to speak, a clear, male voice had said, "Need help!" From this, I knew they could speak in English and, given the circumstances, perhaps the message was appropriate.

The famous alabaster sphinx at Memphis, capitol of the Old Kingdom of Lower Egypt. To the left is an open sarcophagus where the author taped her first message in Egypt.

Although I seldom record "Help!" messages now, when I first began taping, hundreds of this nature were received. While preparing for my trip to Egypt, I had the suspicion that if I was successful in recording anything, and could understand what was said, it would be from what are known as earthbound spirits who had not been able to make a transition into the world after death.

This suspicion was only slightly borne out during the remainder of our stay. My daughter, Becky, who went with me, and I taped well over 100 messages. Less than five requested our help. Becky, who was taping for the first time, had excellent results. At the Temple of Abydos, while sitting in a room by herself, she received almost a minute of beautiful singing. Although it is difficult to say how many voices were involved, from the volume one would have to estimate at least five or six. Out of all the messages taped, this is the only one that appears to be in an archaic language and I believe it is in a tongue unknown to man.

It is interesting, though, that they began their message to Becky in English with, "We are loving." A minute later, after the untranslatable singing, they reverted back to English with, "We are serving. You will serve." It should be stressed that there was no singing at Abydos while we were there.

It was also at Abydos where I received a memorable message. After ending with the usual, "We ask for your blessing," a clear voice replied, "Got your blessing!"

Voices were taped each day during our visit. They came through to me during a late-night vigil at the Sphinx. I heard from them at the Beni Hassan tombs on top of a steep cliff. At the Temple of Dendera in a room used for magic rites thousands of years ago, a male voice called me by name and said, "Sarah. Please guide me. I love."

They were with me out in the Western Desert where there are hundreds of Coptic tombs, most only partly standing after more than 1,000 years. There a clear, female voice told me, "I buried you." Could I have returned to the scene of a previous burial from an earlier life lived in Egypt? At a small tomb near the Great Pyramid, different voices spoke, saying they talked to me with love; they knew I'd come; they were back with me; and, "My mother."

During two following trips to Egypt, voices continued speaking through my tape recorder. At several locations entities who spoke on our first visit returned with additional messages.

## Taping in England

In June 1988, I helped lead a metaphysical group to England for 12 days. During our stay, I taught an EVP workshop on location to those in the group who were interested. Many people were thrilled to discover that they too had made contact with the invisibles through their recorders.

Our first stop was at Beaulieu Abbey, formerly a monastery, later a stately home. I paused by the family grave of the people who had once owned Beaulieu and invited Victoria, the name on one of the headstones, to speak. A clear female voice replied, "Yes, I went home."

At Tintagel Castle, the legendary castle of King Arthur and Merlin, located on the wild and windswept Cornish coast, I sat on an outcrop of stones gazing down at the crashing surf and Merlin's cave. My own name "Sarah" was taped at this time. The voice, showing the quality of location as these voices frequently do, sounded as if it was coming from a great distance away.

Much closer contact was made at Stonehenge. I moved out into the field away from the crowd but still facing the stones. I asked how the unseen felt about the current state of Stonehenge. A male voice, sounding as if he was by my shoulder, told me, "Now I am gone."

We stopped at Warwick Castle, one of the finest medieval castles in Britain. Built in the 12th century and perfectly preserved, it has a long history of many hauntings. I took my recorder, and the others who were taping, down into the dungeon. Prisoners were kept in deplorable conditions and as part of the room, a small hole had been hollowed out of the ground. This was where especially despised prisoners were kept. Lowering my recorder as much as possible into the hole, I said I hoped they had found the peace they sought. A male voice answered, "I love you, my friend."

## Voices from Italy

Near the end of May 1989, I was invited to lecture about my work in taping voices at the international conference held by the Centro Milanese Metafonia organization in Milan, Italy. At the conclusion of the conference, I went to Rome for four days and visited the usual well-known historical locations.

On the first morning, I went to the Vatican and St. Peter's Church. Sitting quietly in the sanctuary, I explained softly to the unseen that I was holding a tape recorder in my hand and could record their words if they wished to speak. Immediately some said, "Recording," followed a moment later with, "We like you."

## Tapes from the dead

Similar messages were taped at the Coliseum. As I walked around the mossy, grass-covered tiers of still partly remaining seats where the early Romans sat while watching the games, I had mixed feelings. I sensed desperation, fear, happy excitement and some guilt. This was no doubt due to the emotional differences existing between the spectators and those they had come to watch. Again, I explained what I was holding in my hand and what it could do. A loud voice said, "Recorder," followed with, "We love you."

At the catacombs of St. Domitilla, I left the group and went into a small side room where there were candles and a cross. Inviting those to speak who were present, two messages came through. The first, a male voice said, "We will come." This was followed by a female voice who added, "With her. I go with her."

## A mystery with Poe

Numerous other recordings have been made out in the field but closer to home. A somewhat amusing but baffling incident occurred while I was sitting on a stone bench beside the tombstone of Edgar Allan Poe who is buried in Baltimore at the Westminster Church. *Evening Magazine*, Philadelphia, had contacted me about doing a special which showed me taping voices. A full day was planned. That morning we had gone to a haunted mansion in Baltimore, and I taped several voices. The afternoon was set aside for Poe's house three blocks away, where Poe lived at one time. Everything was going well at the gravesite. I held up my tape recorder, explaining it was not necessary to have elaborate, expensive equipment in order to tape voices. I went on to mention some of the messages I had taped lately, including one in which I had been assured that our beloved pets survived death and we would see them again.

Suddenly, out of nowhere, a small, nondescript cat jumped up on the bench and sat down beside me. No one had seen it coming – it was just there! The cameraman was so shocked, as was everyone else, that he failed to get it on film. I wish I could say it dematerialized in front of us but no, after several seconds it jumped off the bench and stalked away with catly dignity. The animal was solid, for I gave it a hug. If it was a ghost cat, it had done a good job of materialization!

## Back to Westminster

In August 1987, I returned to the Westminster Church. With me was a group that had signed up for the workshop I was teaching as part of the national conference for my organization, the American Association-Electronic Voice Phenomena. Everyone carried a portable tape recorder and our plan was to first visit the catacomb under the church to try to tape voices and then go to the Poe House.

The cemetery and grounds, dating back to the 1700s, is the oldest in Baltimore. I tried to prepare the group ahead of time for the catacomb.

It is a large, dark, damp, dismal room, an ideal setting for a horror film. A few caskets are lying behind iron grills, with the others scattered around the room. There have been numerous reports of apparitions and other unexplainable happenings, and one can sense being in the presence of the unquiet dead. The room is almost overwhelming, and one needs fortitude to proceed.

Feeling great compassion for the perceived scores of unhappy ghosts, the group and I separated, each person walking around taping where he or she wished. Several of us had results. In my own case, out of the five messages I taped, the most unusual, as well as disquieting, was a clear male voice that said, "We leave the soul right down here."

## Woodrow Wilson

Two years ago, a producer at WTTG Channel 5 of Washington, DC called and said they would like to film me trying to tape voices at President Woodrow Wilson's house. The house, a stately mansion nearly 100 years old, is located on Embassy Row in Washington. Although the house has not been lived in for over 20 years, it is open to the public at certain hours for tours. Several people work there daily to keep the fully furnished house in a fine state of preservation.

The staff has reported many cases of unexplained phenomena. An apparition of a woman is often seen gliding down the stairs; footsteps are heard pacing back and forth; and voices and laughter come from empty rooms.

Arrangements were made by WTTG for me to visit the house one evening when all visitors were gone. During the three hours I spent in the house, I taped several excellent quality voices. They were all received in President Wilson's bedroom as I held the recorder above the bed where he spent many months as a result of ill health.

At the beginning of the taping, when I asked if anyone was present, a male voice whispered, "I'm here." Two seconds later the same voice, but louder, added, "I miss the children." An hour later, after walking through the house, I returned to the bedroom. This time, in answer to my question as to whether there was anyone on the bed, a female voice answered, "Just Swaden: Something's trying to pull him."

No claim is made that I was in contact with President Wilson or his wife Edith, who lived in the house until 1961. The house was occupied by others before the Wilsons bought it in the 1920s.

## "Free to go on"
Taping voices away from home has added a new dimension to my work. At times I have been able to return to the scene of a previous recording, such as the sarcophagus at Memphis, and the Temple of Dendera, where I had received requests for help. When this occurs, I gently explain what has happened. I tell them many years have passed since their death. Their job here is finished and they are free to go on. I say they will find friends, loved ones and other friendly spirits waiting for them. They will find great happiness and expanded opportunities if they go, and I suggest they look for a bright light and move in that direction. Upon occasion, a final message has come through from the individual I am trying to help, indicating that they have, in fact, seen the light and are going toward it.

## Not all lost souls
Originally, I thought that all voices taped in the field would be "lost" souls. I now know this is not true. I have learned that it largely depends on where one tapes. Many messages have been received in historical places indicating, I believe, that I was in contact with what is known as an "advanced" soul. You should know something about the history of where you are taping. When you get there, focus your questions on that situation. If it is within you, it may help if you have empathy for those you want to contact.

## Basic taping instructions
It is not difficult to record voices. In every EVP workshop I have taught on location, results were achieved often by people taping for the first time. You need not be a psychic superstar to receive voices on tape. Move away from the crowds. Find a quiet spot. Be aware of cold spots. I make a practice of first assuring the unseen that I come in friendship and in peace, and that I mean them no harm. Carefully, I explain that I am only going to be there a short time. Remember, when taping in a haunted location, you are in a place that a ghost regards as his home. You have walked in uninvited but more than likely the spirit will be tolerant of your visit as long as it knows you're not going to be around forever.

Wherever you tape, you have a good chance of success. Pick up your portable tape recorder, put a 60-minute tape in, make sure your batteries are fresh, and walk out the door!

*Sarah Estep (d. 2008): One of the pioneers in EVP research, author and founder of the American Association-EVP, now Association TransCommunication. Even after the advent of digital recorders, Estep preferred magnetic tape, including her original reel-to-reel setup.*

FATE May 1991

# NEW APPROACHES TO COMMUNICATION
# BEYOND THE GRAVE
## Gregory J. Lapkoff

An amazing group of scientists and lay people gathered in Chicago for a conference sponsored by The Noetic Sciences Foundation, an organization founded by Edgar Mitchell, the sixth man to walk on the surface of the moon. The conference drew hundreds of attendees from all over the world. As a former member of the Noetic Sciences Foundation, I was invited. The meeting was organized as a series of workshops, with the topics of life, death and the survival of consciousness as recurring themes.

My own tour of the conference began with a keynote address and welcome by Dr. Raymond Moody, famous for his near-death research. It was Dr. Moody who coined the term "near-death experience," when he wrote his first best-selling book, *Life After Life.*

## Reunions in the psychomanteum

Dr. Moody's discussion centered on his discovery that gazing into a mirror in a particular way can evoke the dramatic appearance of an apparition of a deceased person.

Moody, who refers to himself as a non-parapsychologist, opened his talk by telling us that when we heard what he had to say, we would think that he had lost his mind. He quickly cautioned, however, that "only those who lose their minds can find them."

Moody, who has a philosophy background in addition to his psychiatric credentials, came upon his mirror-gazing idea while he was reminiscing about a mythology course he had taken. He particularly remembered the stories of the ancient oracles of the dead at Ephyra, and the Greeks' methods of gazing into calm waters, cauldrons and even pools of blood to evoke the spirits.

Comparing this mythology with his own belief that humans are prone to apparitional encounters, Moody decided that the mythological descriptions were real and not poetic fantasy.

Setting about to prove his hypothesis, Moody constructed what he called a psychomanteum, a room that had black drapery on every wall and on the ceiling. A single chair sat in the center. One wall was graced by a mirror, angled in such a way that when Moody was seated in the chair, he could not see his own reflection. Instead he viewed a "clear optical depth," an infinity, really, that he gazed into. The whole room was illuminated only by a 15-watt bulb positioned behind the chair.

Dr. Moody gathered several volunteers to try his gazing experiment. The results were spectacular. Fifty per cent of the gazers had an apparitional contact; of these, 15 per cent had the experience of having an apparition emerge from the mirror. Even more incredible was that 25 per cent had further apparitional encounters in places other than the psychomanteum.

When Moody interviewed the first volunteers, he thought that they were being confused by visual hallucinations. But each person he spoke to insisted that the experience was real. It was then that Moody decided to try it himself. If anyone could determine what was illusion and what was real, it would be a psychiatrist.

Moody's experience turned out to be one of the most notable of all. Three weeks after his mirror gazing session, he was sitting alone. A woman he did not immediately recognize entered the room. The woman turned out to be the "ghost" of his dead grandmother. He made direct eye contact with her. She talked at length about incidents from his childhood, and they resolved some old differences. In Moody's own words, "death had done her a world of good."

Parapsychologist Jeffrey Mishlove feels that Moody's new work may represent one of the most exciting breakthroughs in survival research in this century. For the first time ever, scientists will be able to induce or create the manifestation of genuine apparitions. It will remain to be seen whether or not more than one person at a time can see the same apparition.

Moody himself makes no claims as to the meaning or importance of his work. He just says that the results are interesting.

In closing, Moody said that he believed that we would never scientifically prove a life after death. Every time we get close to such a proof, the goal line gets pushed back. When people first started being resuscitated after heart failure and respiratory cessation, for example, they began to tell strange, compelling stories of the near-death experience. Doctors and scientists countered that these people were not really dead, and thus they could shed no true life on the after-death experience. They were dead, however, by the standards of a few years earlier. So, the goal line had been pushed back. It is a goal line that Moody feels will always recede as fast as proofs of life after death emerge. For Moody, the proof of life after death will always remain a personal one.

## Transcommunication with the dead

Mark Macy and the other experimenters in transcommunication, or direct instrumental contact with the dead, do not agree that the only proof of life after death will be one's personal experience. This group claims direct post mortem contact via telephone, television, computer and other electronic communication devices, including fax machines.

Macy gave a presentation called, "When Dimensions Cross: High Tech Communication with the Spirits of the Dead." Macy represents the American arm of a fairly large group of lay people, scientists and technicians who claim to be in direct electronic contact with the dead. This work is the direct evolution of electronic voice phenomena (EVP) popularized during the 1970s.

Macy said that human beings all possess several bodies, including the physical body and several nonphysical bodies. In addition, there exist many planes of existence, including the physical plane, the lower, middle and upper astral planes and the causal planes.

In the middle astral planes, said Macy, there exists a world that closely resembles the Earth. On this world a tremendous river, the River of Eternity, loops the surface. It is to this world that most of us go when we die, and it is from this world that the spirits communicating are originating.

Macy showed videotapes of several of the spirit-side people involved. They were not pictures and tapes of them when they were alive, but after they died. These images are the crux of a controversy. We are either watching an incredibly bold fraud, or we are watching a major development of the 20th century unfolding before our eyes.

Macy's videos showed 19th-century explorer Sir Richard Francis Burton slowly moving his head to and fro. He appeared to be dark-haired and handsome, and he did resemble paintings I have seen of the real Burton. But what is real here?

Next to be seen was Konstantin Raudive, famous for his early electronic voice experimentation, and dead since 1974. It looked like Raudive all right – he was wearing the same glasses that he wore in physical life. Macy played an audio tape of his own telephone contact with Raudive. We heard Raudive's booming, heavily accented voice announcing that an electronic bridge is now being established to the US. It is up to Macy and others, such as experimenter George Meek, said Raudive's voice, to strengthen the bridge.

After Raudive's statements, the video showed us Thomas Edison, who died in 1931, and director George Cukor, also deceased, standing together, wearing suits and ties.

My mind reeled, but Macy was not through. Seventeenth-century physician Paracelsus popped up on the screen. Then a person named Swejan Salter (who never lived on Earth) appeared next to him. Then a man appeared wrapped in gauze like a mummy, wearing some sort of gloves and goggles over his eyes.

"Who is that guy?" someone asked.

Mark told us that this was an advanced being named Technician who never had a physical life and who always appears this way on video.

Technician is the entity who heads up a team of spirits on the astral plane, 1,000 strong, all dedicated to establishing communication with Earth. I imagined sort of a Project Apollo of spirits, all working to make a metaphorical landing on Earth.

The audience was buzzing with questions. "Why do spirits wear ties and glasses?" "Have you made a video contact here in the States?"

I asked Macy why his story of the Riverworld so closely parallels the science fiction stories of Phillip Jose Farmer.

Macy answered many of the questions. Neither he nor any other American experimenter has made a video contact. The bridge is not yet strong enough, he claims, and requires more people to become involved. He also told us that skeptical attitudes interfere with communication. Spirits wear glasses and such things because that is what they became accustomed to on Earth. He could not explain why his story closely resembled the works of Farmer but suggested that perhaps I should contact the science fiction writer.

## Science and life after death

Jeffrey Mishlove was interested in a career in criminology. One night as he slept in his room at the University California at Berkley campus he dreamed of his uncle back home in the Midwest. In the dream, his uncle disagreed with the path that young Jeffrey had chosen. Soon after, Mishlove contacted his parents and inquired about his uncle. He was informed that his relative had just died.

This startling dream sent Mishlove down far different a path than he had planned. Mishlove earned a PhD in parapsychology. He has since written several books, including *The Roots of Consciousness,* and he is the current host of the acclaimed television series *Thinking Allowed.* Dr. Mishlove's workshop was entitled "Scientific Evidence for the Survival of Personality After Death."

In his lively presentation, Mishlove wove a tapestry of evidence supporting life after death. He showed the immensity of evidence, which ranged from NDEs to the mathematical theories of hyperspace. He chose to spend much time, however, on the famous cross-correspondences that occurred earlier this century.

I thought that this would be old hat and I was anxious to hear more about hyperspace. Mishlove, however, pointed out that the cross-correspondences represent some of the most compelling evidence of life after death.

The cross-correspondence cases were a series of communications (a multitude really) received piecemeal by a group of mediums, many times unknown to each other, in the early 20th century. The message pieces made no sense whatsoever unless they were linked to other messages received by other communicators; hence "cross-correspondences." At least seven mediums from the US, India and England were involved. Adding to the complexities was the fact that many of the messages were received in a sort of complex code utilizing classical Greek literature references.

The purported communicators included F.W.H. Myers, one of the founders of the Society for Psychical Research in London, and the classical Greek scholar behind the puzzles being "transmitted." These communications went on for 23 years and contain over 3,000 messages. Many were deciphered. Volumes of messages are still filed away, awaiting the proper scholar to decipher their hidden links and meanings.

Mishlove went on to build his case, mixing in examples of possessions, OBEs, reincarnation studies and hyperspace theories.

## A trip through hyperspace

Hyperspace is a mathematical construct that was first conceptualized by physicist Saul Paul Sirag. It is a meaningful breakthrough in survival research because it is the first hard mathematical concept that can be said to scientifically allow for the survival of the human personality after death. In fact, it may be a mathematical description of the astral planes that we hear so much about.

Basically, the math of hyperspace proposes that existence extends into more than just the three physical dimensions – height, width and depth – that we experience daily. There are many unseen dimensional spaces that we do not experience with our physical senses. Conversely, our physical body may exist only as a minor extension of our full, multi-dimensional self into the physical plane. Upon death we lose the physical body and withdraw our consciousness into a more expansive existence in hyperspace. Mishlove theorizes that we may actually be experiencing hyperspace in certain dreams, particularly lucid dreams.

One of the staunchest critics of all things psychic, CSICOP (Committee for the Scientific Investigation of Claims of the Paranormal) member Martin Gardner admits that hyperspace allows for the possibility of survival of the human personality after death. Mishlove believes that our future descendants will explore the landscapes of hyperspace just as we once explored the Earth, and as we are now exploring outer space.

I walked away from Mishlove's presentation and the conference with a new respect for the survival hypothesis. Brick by brick, it seemed that a magnificent edifice was being built, an edifice that the skeptics could not so easily tear down, proving that there is more to us than our physical existence.

FATE February 1995

# PHONE CALLS FROM THE DEAD
## Rosemary Ellen Guiley

One night on Open Lines on *Coast to Coast AM,* host George Noory took a call from a woman named "Wilma" (pseudonym) who said she was convinced she had received a telephone call from her mother – after she died.

Wilma's mother had been gravely ill for some time. One night when Wilma was home, her phone rang around three in the morning. Three AM is a time when many mysterious and paranormal events take place, and one was about to happen to Wilma. When she answered, she heard static that sounded like a voice struggling to get through on the other end but was not saying anything intelligible. Puzzled, she hung up. Shortly thereafter Wilma's sister called and informed her that their mother had died at about the same time as the static call. Wilma was convinced her mother was on the other end when she picked up the phone and was trying to get through a lot of static to let her know that she had passed on and all was well.

Experiences like that can send shivers down a spine. It's one thing to get messages from the dead relayed through a psychic or medium and another to hear the voice of a dead person with your own ears over the telephone. How can a person who has left life on earth, and who no longer has a physical body and vocal chords, make use of earthly technology? Does a phone call from a dead person prove survival after death?

We can see from the history of high tech spirit communications – electronic voice phenomena (EVP) and instrumental transcommunication (ITC) – that the dead have been making use of whatever technology we have had available to pierce the veil. How the disembodied can reach out from realms we cannot see or experience, and operate our equipment, is at the core of the mystery of spirit communications.

## Taking the calls seriously

Phone calls from the dead did not get much attention until the 1960s, when paranormal researchers began investigating them. In 1967, D. Scott Rogo and Raymond Bayless, who were studying mediums, were invited to a seance where the hostess told them a friend of hers had received a phone call from her dead son. The son said, "Hello Mother?" and then the line went dead. The woman had positively recognized the voice of her son.

To Rogo and Bayless, the story seemed far-fetched. It must have been a fluke wrong number from a man who sounded like the woman's son. They wondered aloud how such a call could be proved, and then let the matter drop.

But it didn't end there. Rogo and Bayless found themselves coming across more accounts of phone calls from the dead – so many, in fact, that they could no longer ignore the phenomenon. They decided they had to investigate. They had no shortage of cases and people to interview. Referrals came to them from other prominent researchers, among them Gertrude Schmeidler, who had done significant scientific research of extrasensory perception.

Rogo and Bayless spent three years collecting more than 70 cases and became convinced themselves that phone calls from the dead are genuine. Their results, published in *Phone Calls from the Dead* (1979) was one of the first major books devoted to this unusual phenomenon. Since then, their work has helped many people validate and understand telephonic after-death communications.

## Characteristics of phone calls from the dead

The great majority of phone calls from the dead are exchanges between persons who shared a close emotional tie while both were living, such as parents and children, siblings, other relatives, and close friends.

Many are "intention" calls, initiated by the deceased to impart a message, such as farewell upon death, a warning of impending danger, or information the living person needs to carry out a task. For example, actress Ida Lupino's father, Stanley, who died intestate in London during World War II, called Lupino six months after his death to relate information concerning his estate: the location of some unknown but important papers.

Most calls occur soon after a person has died, usually within 24 hours up to a week. Those calls tend to be short. Longer calls usually come from those who have been dead several months. One of the longest intervals on record is two years.

There may be no communication, just odd static, or the recognizable voice of the dead person may say a few words. There is often a sense of urgency to the call. The callers do not announce they have died, but sometimes they do say they are all right, which mystifies the recipients if they have not yet received news of the death.

Some calls occur on emotionally charged anniversary days, such as Mother's Day, Father's Day, weddings, birthdays, holidays and the anniversary of the dead person's passing. In a typical anniversary call, the dead may do nothing more than repeat a phrase over and over, such as "Hello, Mom, is that you?"

Such calls have been documented for decades. On Mother's Day 1943, a woman named Mary Cahill of New York received a phone call from her daughter Peggy, who had died six months earlier at age 12. Cahill clearly recognized the voice of her dead child, who said, "Hello Mom! How are you? Can you hear me? Hello Mom!" Cahill recounted in her testimony in the September 1953 issue of FATE magazine that trying to talk to Peggy was like "talking through a storm" and "a rushing as of great winds." Suddenly the winds crescendoed to a roar, and the phone line went silent. Cahill called the operator and asked for a trace, but the operator said there was no record of an incoming call to Cahill's number.

In a minority of cases, the call is placed person-to-person, long-distance with the assistance of a mysterious operator. Checks with the telephone company later turn up no evidence of a call being placed.

195

Today, a caller ID may appear on a recipient's phone screen; or, "Private Number," "Unknown Number" or "Out of Area" might appear. In the earlier cases that involved long distance operators, the operators could not trace or verify the originating numbers.

Persons who have received phone calls from the dead report that the voice sounds the same as when the deceased was living; furthermore, the voice uses nicknames and words that readily identified them to the recipients.

The telephone usually rings normally, although some recipients say that the ring sounds flat and abnormal. In many cases, the connection is bad, with a great deal of static, buzzing, popping and line noise, and occasionally the faint voices of other persons are heard, as though lines have been crossed. In many cases, the voice of the dead one is difficult to hear and grows fainter as the call goes on. Sometimes, the voice just fades completely but the line remains open, and the recipient hangs up after giving up on further communication. Sometimes the call is terminated by the dead, and the recipient hears the click of disengagement; other times, the line simply goes dead.

Some phone calls from the dead occur months or even years after the person has died. In one case cited by Rogo and Bayless, an 82-year-old woman who had no telephone while alive was on the other end of a call received by an acquaintance several months after the elderly woman died. All she said was the recipient's name over and over again, until her voice faded completely away.

The phone calls typically occur when the recipient is in a passive state of mind. If the recipient knows the caller is dead, the shock is great and the phone call very brief; the caller terminates the call after a few seconds or minutes, or the line goes dead. If the recipient does not know the caller is dead, a lengthy conversation of up to 30 minutes or so may take place, during which the recipient is not aware of anything amiss.

An example of a lengthy phone call from the dead is recounted by psychical researcher Susy Smith in *The Power of the Mind* (1975). Smith was passionately interested in finding evidence of survival after death, and in communication with the Other Side. The case involves a couple, Bonnie and C.E. McConnell, who lived in Tucson. They were close friends with an elderly woman, identified by the pseudonym of Enid. Enid had once been wealthy, but in the last years of her life did not have enough money to pay for increasingly expensive health care. She moved around from facility to facility as her health waned, and eventually the McConnells lost touch with her. A year went by, and then one Sunday evening they received a phone call from her. Not only were the McConnells surprised to hear from Enid, they were also surprised that her voice sounded so healthy. She seemed vibrant and in good spirits. Enid commented that it was a shame that she hadn't been able to see the McConnells. She told them where she was in Tucson.

Bonnie remembered that Enid's birthday was only two days away and promised to visit Enid and bring her a bottle of her favorite blackberry brandy. "I don't need it now," Enid replied. Bonnie said she would bring it anyway.

The rest of the incident is told in Bonnie's own words, as given to Smith:

> I mentioned that she sounded as if everything was great with her. She said, "It is. I've never had such good care." She also said, "Wasn't it too bad we didn't get that book finished?" I said, "You will," for she sounded absolutely wonderful. After the call, my husband, who had been participating in the conversation, from the bedroom phone, said, "That sounded like the Enid of 20 years ago."
>
> Among other things, I said to Enid, "Do you have a phone by your bed again?" And she replied, "No." Then I said, "Do you mean you can get up and go to the phone?" And she said, "Oh, I can get around fine." I commented that she sounded so happy and she said, "I've never been happier."

The two women talked for about 30 minutes, Bonnie recalled, and they reminisced about old times. The McConnells hung up feeling happy, too.

On Friday of the same week, Bonnie telephoned the nursing home where Enid said she was living and asked to speak to her. The receptionist was shocked. She informed Bonnie that Enid had died on Sunday morning – the same day that the McConnells had gotten the phone call, which had come several hours after her passing.

The McConnells were equally shocked. Both husband and wife had spoken to Enid, had recognized her voice and verified her identity, and had conversed with her as though she were living.

In several cases studied by researchers, the deceased callers make reference to an anonymous "they" who have allowed the communication to take place, and caution that there is little time to talk. The remarks imply that communication between the living and the dead is not only difficult, but not necessarily desirable.

In a small number of cases, the callers are strangers who say they are calling on behalf of a third party, whom the recipients later discover is dead.

Sometimes phone calls from the dead make the news. One such case involved the tragic head-on collision of a Union Pacific freight train and a Metrolink commuter train in the Chatsworth district of Los Angeles at 4:22 PM on Friday, September 12, 2008. Twenty-five people were killed and 135 were injured. Among the casualties was a 49-year-old man named Greg S. (name has been changed) of Salt Lake City. He was in Southern California to interview for a job. He was traveling to his fiancee's house in Westlake Village when the crash occurred. Greg was sitting in the front passenger car where many of the fatalities occurred. Sadly, he was only one stop away from his fiancee when the collision happened.

Greg's body was recovered around 4:30 AM on Saturday, and an autopsy revealed that he had been killed instantly. But for 11 hours following the crash, Greg's family – his son, brother, stepmother, sister and fiancee – received a total 35 calls from his cell phone, up until 3:28 AM. They knew the calls came from Greg's cell phone because of his caller ID. All they heard was static and vague sounds, and they received no response to their questions and words of encouragement. They had no idea that Greg had already perished, and held out the hope that he was still alive and was trying to reach them. Who made the calls? How did they happen? No one had an explanation.

## Voice mails

In addition to making phone calls, the dead also leave messages on answering machines and voice mail. Konstantin Raudive was known to leave messages on the answering machines and voice mails of key ITC researchers, who recognized his distinctive voice; he often identified himself.

The two cases below, from the research literature, demonstrate phone call messages that seem to have the purpose of reassurance and an ongoing, unbroken bond with the living.

In April 1986, the father of a woman named Ophelia passed away, and his death was hard on her older brother. Months later, her brother started a new job. One day soon after he began, he arrived at work and was handed a message from the switchboard. It said, "Your father called." He questioned the operator, who said the call had come in just minutes before he had arrived, and the caller said, "Just tell him his father called."

Another example of a message comes from a woman named Suzie, who lost a dear friend early in 2009. A few months later, she was startled at a voice mail she received. There were sounds of a great deal of static, and then a voice she clearly recognized as that of her friend said, "I made it Suzie." Suzie was elated. She had wished for a sign from her friend that she was all right, and the voice mail confirmed that to her.

## Making phone calls to the dead

Phone calls *to* the dead are as equally mysterious as phone calls from the dead. In some cases, a living person calls someone not knowing that person has died. The dead person answers the call.

One example reported by Stanley R. Dean in *Psychiatry and Mysticism* (1975) featured a New Jersey resident named Maria D'Alessio. One night, D'Alessio had a vivid, disturbing dream in which a childhood friend named Lana sank into a pool of blood. She had not been in touch with Lana in some time, so the next day D'Alessio called her to make certain her friend was all right. Lana answered and acknowledged that she had been sick and had even been in the hospital. In fact, she was due to return to the hospital the following day. D'Alessio said she would come and visit her there, but Lana discouraged the idea, saying she would call D'Alessio later. No call ever came. D'Alessio called Lana repeatedly but no one ever answered the phone. Finally, she found out that Lana had died *six months earlier.* Her widowed husband told D'Alessio that she must have been mistaken about talking to his dead wife.

## Explaining phone calls from the dead

How do we explain phone calls from the dead? Three main explanations have been put forward. One is that they are what they seem to be – phone calls between the dead and the living. A second is that the calls are a psychokinesis (PK) effect unwittingly produced by the living. Psychokinesis, the influence of mind over matter, has been demonstrated in laboratory experiments. And, there are many cases of unwitting psychokinesis, such as poltergeist effects, which seem to be caused by a psychic projection or explosion of emotional energy or tension. In the case of phone calls from the dead, emotional energy such as shock and grief would be the apparent causes of the PK. The voice of the dead person would then be an artificial creation of the projected energy.

A possible example of intense emotional projection can be seen in a case reported in FATE in January 1960. Ruth Pritchard of Denver related a strange call received on her first birthday following the death of her son in October 1957. She was extremely sad on that day – until a mysterious phone call came. She recognized the voice of her dead son, who said one word, "Mom?" There was a click and the call ended. Pritchard felt that the call had come in answer to her "heartfelt prayer."

But the PK explanation is a stretch and cannot explain all phone calls from the dead. In most cases, the living recipient does not know the caller is dead – so how could they project enough emotion to cause PK? And, if emotion and grief from the living can create these types of calls, then they would be more commonplace. Yearning for the voice of a departed loved one is a powerful emotion.

A third explanation is that the calls are caused by some unknown cosmic trickster. It is true that trickster elements appear in all aspects of the paranormal, so this cannot be ruled out. Would such cruel jokes be played on the grieving living? It is more likely that there is an unknown explanation for how and why phone calls bridging two dimensions can take place.

One question that puzzles psychical researchers concerns the point of origin of the calls. Do they really come from another dimension? Or do the dead manipulate forces in our dimension? Is there an actual device, like a phantom telephone, on the Other Side or in another dimension? If the calls are a form of energy, why do they seem to need a device on our end?

Paranormal researcher Tom Slemen of England documented an odd case that occurred in 1995 and which pointed to calls originating in this dimension. A popular medium, James Byrne, was a guest on a Liverpool radio show, giving messages from the dead to callers. One caller, identified as Mrs. Wilson, wanted a message from her dead grandfather but could not get through on the jammed phone lines. A few hours after the show was over, Mrs. Wilson received a phone call – from her grandfather. Speaking as though from a great distance, he said, "Look love, I'm all right. It's great over here; I'm with your grandmother and all the other nice people who have passed on."

Dumbfounded, Mrs. Wilson said, "Granddad, is that you?"

He answered, "Yeah love. Now listen: stop living in the past and reminiscing. Go forward. I'm still around looking over you. I've got to go now, love. Give my love to the kids. Bye." His voice then faded away.

At first Mrs. Wilson thought someone must be playing a terrible joke on her, even though no one else knew she had been trying to call Byrnes while he was on the show. She called the phone company to get the caller's number. The automated response was almost as astonishing as the call itself – the call had come from her own phone number!

How could a call from her own number ring her phone? It is impossible to call yourself on your own phone. Try it. Had Granddad on the Other Side somehow manipulated an unknown force or energy to generate the call from within Mrs. Wilson's own equipment? No one can answer that question for certain, but researchers in EVP have also speculated that EVP recordings may, in at least some cases, originate internally in the equipment of the living. In the case of phone calls, we hear in the earpiece whatever is generated over the microphone inside the telephone's receiver. Thus, according to this possible explanation, the mystery caller would have to register a voice on the microphone in order for the recipient to hear it.

And what about the other telephone sounds, such as the ringer, dial tone, and the click heard when a call is terminated? Some or all of those so-called normal sounds are present in phone calls from the dead.

One of the cases from the files of German parapsychologist Hans Bender featured an abnormal ring. On January 30, 1978, the telephone of a young man rang in an odd "deadened" way. The caller on the other end was his father, who had died four years earlier. His voice repeated several times, "I am here, Daddy... here, Daddy," and then asked, "How is Mommy, how is Mommy?" The call abruptly terminated.

There are a few odd cases in which the phantom phone calls were placed by unknown persons who had information about a known person and calls in which mystery persons interrupted a call. Alfred Hitchcock wrote about one such case in 1955 in *Coronet* magazine. In January 1934, the mother of a man named Arne Gandy was hoping to hear from her son, who was in San Francisco. At 3 AM one morning, the phone rang. Mrs. Gandy had an unlisted number, so she immediately thought it must be her son. Instead, she heard a strange man's voice. "The kid is here, and for God's sake forgive him and give him another chance. What I said about him in my letter is all true, he is a fine kid."

The caller declined to identify himself. Mrs. Gandy said he had the wrong number, for she had no letter and did not know what he was talking about. He repeated her correct, unlisted number. Several voices came over the line. Mrs. Gandy asked to speak to her son. The voices laughed, and the mystery man said, "Your son is in a hospital in San Francisco. He's in bad shape. But never mind, he is on his way home now." Another voice said, "I am helpless. Here I lie propped up on pillows. I can't move." The voice sighed and groaned, and the call faded away.

The next morning, Arne's body was found in San Francisco Bay. He had drowned about two days prior and was dead at the time the call had been placed.

Another case reported in *Tomorrow* magazine (once published by the famous medium Eileen J. Garrett) was of a call from Tom, who was a man dying in a hospital in 1954. The call was made to a friend, who thought the man was now recovering instead of being at death's door. He sounded bright and chipper, full of energy. The call was interrupted by a mystery man who said he wanted to talk to Tom and would reconnect the call when he was through. The promised call never came.

Such calls raise additional questions about the process and mechanisms of phone calls from the dead. Do others on the Other Side monitor, help or hinder such calls? If so, who are they? Others who are dead? Angels or spirit beings? We still have more questions than answers.

*[Adapted from articles,* The Encyclopedia of Ghosts and Spirits *(2008) by Rosemary Ellen Guiley and* Talking to the Dead *(2011) by George Noory and Rosemary Ellen Guiley.]*

Rosemary Ellen Guiley: Author, researcher and Executive Editor of FATE.

# INDUCED AFTER-DEATH
# COMMUNICATION
## K. Martin

"I was hoping to talk to my son, Kyle," Sandra explains. "He had died only two months before of a previously undiagnosed heart condition during basketball practice. According to doctors he had the condition since birth, but nobody ever suspected because he was always perfectly healthy.

"He was only 16 and a star athlete, so there was absolutely no way we could have prepared ourselves for what happened. I never had a chance to say goodbye to him; by the time my husband got in touch with me he had been pronounced dead. I went into a horrible depression over it, sometimes even considering taking my own life because I didn't feel like I could go on.

"I just couldn't accept that he was gone. I thought that if there was an afterlife then I would be with him, and if there wasn't, I wouldn't have to live with his loss anymore."

Sandra eventually heard about a doctor in a nearby city who practiced a technique called Induced After-Death Communication. She was immediately intrigued. Claims made by practitioners sounded like science fiction, but according to people who have experienced the phenomenon, it is real, though unexplainable.

"I thought that maybe if I could at least say goodbye, I would be able to pull myself back together for the sake of my family and give them what they still needed from me," Sandra explains. "What I got out of it was more than I ever could have anticipated. It literally changed my entire perspective on life. It's the most profound experience I think a person could ever have.

"I spoke to Kyle and he told me that he was fine, that I needed to stop grieving and be happy for him because he was very happy. And most of all that my family needed me. Then, right before he left, he touched my hand and told me I was a wonderful mother and I had done everything for him I could.

"I had been grieving so badly that I had withdrawn from everyone, including my husband and my daughter. It was almost like I was dead too, but still somehow stuck inside of my shell of a body... After seeing him I felt a weight was lifted from me. My depression vanished, and it has never returned."

At first the phenomenon of Induced After-Death Communication sounds like something from the TV series *Medium*. A subject grieving the loss of a loved one is led to a state of relaxation and, with the aid of the inducer, is guided to a communication with someone who is no longer living.

These encounters are experienced by many as complete, all-encompassing, multi-sensory communications with the deceased in which the subject is given messages of comfort and frequently new insight into something involving the departed loved one, something that he or she would otherwise have no way of knowing.

As remarkable as this sounds, psychiatrists who are versed in the technique report up to 90 percent success rates in achieving Induced After-Death Communications, or IADCs, for their clients. What's more, trauma associated with the loss of the loved one is invariably very much improved by the experience.

While most psychiatrists who practice IADC are reluctant to claim that these are communications with actual spirits of the dead, they also note that the messages received by the patients frequently go well beyond simple wish fulfillment. Not only is new information given, but in some cases the deceased tells the patient things he or she did not particularly want to hear.

IADC was discovered accidentally by a psychiatrist, Dr. Francine Shapiro. Using rapid eye movements, she found she was able to desensitize herself (and later, her patients) to negative emotions resulting from traumatic memories by first achieving a state of total recall, and then by processing the experience again with the advantage of new experience.

It wasn't long before psychiatrists using the technique discovered something far more puzzling was happening with their patients using the rapid-eye-movement method of accessing memories. Sometimes, when those memories involved someone who had died, the person experienced a seemingly full-fledged communication.

Psychiatrists started comparing notes and found that the phenomenon was reliably reproducible and that it seemed to conform to certain consistent parameters.

Patients began to report the appearance of loved ones who had crossed over. These appearances included conversations and physical contact that were experienced just as if they were happening in real time. In his book *Induced After-Death Communication*, Dr. Allan L. Botkin details many case studies of the phenomenon. He even recounts instances in which he shared in these perceptions with the patients.

Of course, after-death communications have been reported by many people who have grieved the loss of someone close to them. Some experts estimate, based on surveys, that half of all people in Western societies have had some type of experience that they considered a communication from a deceased loved one. The difference with this technique is that it reliably produces these experiences. The quality, duration and intensity of the experience are also much enhanced.

Margaret, a teacher in northern Virginia, spoke about her own experience with IADC: "I was grieving terribly after the death of a good friend. That was my reason for pursuing the therapy. Imagine my surprise when the first person who showed up was a friend from when I was in high school. He died over 20 years ago. I never knew Andrew, though I spent time with him. I never had a conversation with him, though we talked at length to one another.

"Andrew was afflicted with aphasia as a result of head injury sustained when an all-terrain vehicle turned over on him. It had occurred before I met him. His particular aphasia was characterized by extreme verbosity accompanied by complete inability to form meaning with the words that rushed forth like water over a broken levy. It is what linguists sometimes call word salad. A seemingly random verbal output.

"Andrew understood language. If he was asked to go upstairs, for instance, he behaved in ways that made it clear he understood, but communication in the sense of a two-way exchange of ideas was impossible. Since I had never met him before the accident, it was impossible that I could ever really know him. But he showed up at my front door several times during his last couple of months of life, seemingly just wanting to hang around. He talked to me and I talked to him, although I had no idea what he was saying. I had a sense that he just wanted to be understood. That he wanted a little human warmth, although he was quite aware that whatever it was he wanted to say could never be understood.

"It was only a couple of days after his last visit that a mutual friend knocked on the door. When I answered he told me that Andrew was dead. He had taken his own life. I was stunned.

"When I was induced I was met by a middle-aged man, who looked to be fit and happy. At first, I didn't even recognize him. He proceeded to tell me that he had made a mistake in ending his life, which he had done after realizing that he would never have a normal life. He felt he would never be able to have a job, get married or do any of the things that other people took for granted. What he failed to understand, he said, smiling brightly, was that his handicap was something he was supposed to learn from.

"He said that he always felt bad that he hadn't been able to talk with me in a normal way and tell me how much he appreciated my talking to him all those years ago.

"The striking thing about the whole experience was that he looked so well, seemingly radiating inner peace. He told me that everything was really okay for him now and that everyone who passed over, though they might have to deal with the aftermath of something like a suicide, ended up okay. But, he warned me, suicide is always a mistake. The pain you cause others during your life comes back to you and suicide causes great pain."

This is another theme that seems to emerge from the sessions conducted by Dr. Botkin. Suicides never fail to mention that the pain their choice caused was brought back to them, and that proof of the afterlife should not encourage anyone to take their own life; just the opposite, in fact.

"I didn't see the friend I thought I would that day," Margaret continues, "but it really didn't matter. I understood after seeing Andrew that my friend also was okay. One thing though: before the IADC, I wasn't sure I believed in an afterlife. I'm not religious and I never had any sort of metaphysical bent, but now I'm convinced that there is more than this life."

Some skeptics have argued that the nature of the experience is such that only people who are hardcore believers in the first place will bother to seek this therapy. Dr. Botkin, however, has reported trying the therapy on people who have varying degrees of belief, including some that absolutely could not accept the possibility. While there are some people who do not achieve a full IADC, he still reports an astonishing success rate, even with nonbelievers.

*K. Martin: Freelance writer.*

FATE July-August 2008

# SPIRIT FACES: EVIDENCE FROM THE AFTERLIFE
## Rosemary Ellen Guiley

The last act that William Dubs was able to perform before cancer claimed his life was to kiss his soulmate and wife, Tianna Conte-Dubs. As they kissed, he died, and when his soul lifted from his body, Tianna was swept along with him, down a tunnel of light, as though she were dying, too. But she was not meant to cross the final bridge with him, and she returned to her own life, completely shattered at the loss of her greatest love.

In the weeks following William's death, Tianna heard his voice and was comforted, despite a skeptical part of her that insisted that his presence was simply part of her grieving and desire for him to still be alive. Then she got a photo of William from the afterlife, and her own life changed forever.

The photograph, a Polaroid, was taken by Mark Macy, a leading researcher in the frontier field of instrumental transcommunication

(ITC), or high-tech communication in images, voices and text with the dead and higher spiritual realms. Tianna's image was blurred and superimposed upon her face was the unmistakable image of William. His face was clearly recognizable to Tianna and to others who were present. "I was outrageously surprised," said Tianna. "It was the proof I needed that William has survived."

Macy began taking spirit face photographs in 1999 with the purposes of capturing evidence of the existence of other realms and aiding the grieving. His dedication is to "The Project," a post-Atlantean, multi-dimensional effort to bring humans back to God. Through The Project, humans will raise their spiritual consciousness to make a quantum leap into fruitful relationships with higher realms. "I'd like to see us salvage life on Earth and bring Paradise into this world," said Macy. "That's what I've been working for during the past 15 years."

Macy's research and his views on the spiritual destiny of humankind are described in his book *Spirit Faces: Truth About the Afterlife* (2006). The book includes 80 color photographs of spirit face subjects, and many of the personal stories behind them.

## Instant spirit faces

Something remarkable happens when people stand in front of Macy's Polaroid camera. As the photos develop before their eyes, faces of the dead and of unknown entities appear superimposed on the faces of the living. Spirit faces do not manifest every time for everyone, but when they do, they often change worldviews and lives. Skepticism about survival and the existence of higher realms falls away. "I'm forever changed because of this," said Meme Stevens, of Richmond, Virginia. Stevens' photograph showing two spirit faces superimposed on her face – a young man and an older woman, believed to be two of her spirit guides – is on the cover of *Spirit Faces*. "I have a new direction and a new purpose to help raise spiritual awareness," she said.

What makes these faces appear? The spirit faces seem to be facilitated by the presence of a subtle energy device called a luminator, invented by Patrick Richards of Michigan. There are only nine luminators in existence, and all but Macy's are used in psychotherapy. Macy acquired his luminator in 1999, programmed specifically for spirit photography.

The luminator looks like a large, slim stereo speaker. Inside is a Plexiglas barrel lined with rings filled with water-based liquid that acts like crystal, and two counter-rotating fans that pull air into the unit at the bottom and blow it out at the top, creating a vortex within the device.

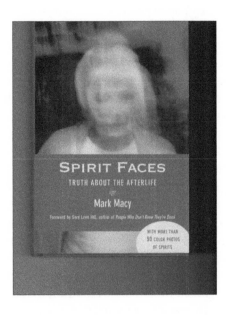

Exactly how the luminator works is not known, but its specific subtle energy programming apparently enables the device to change environmental vibrations in a room. This creates a "noise" matrix for spirits to make impressions on film. "There are many dimensions that are superimposed on ours," said Macy. "They are separated by vibrational level, not by distance or time. We can perceive them when we tune in to their vibrations, just like you would tune in a radio or television frequency. The luminator seems to help us do that."

A spirit face photo is blurry, as though dimensional realms are intersecting. Spirit faces can be full or partial. Macy has experimented with different lighting and environments and has found low indoor light to be the most effective. Sunlight washes out the effects.

It is not known what factors determine whether or not faces appear. For example, several photos can be taken of the same individual, consecutively or at different times, and not all will show spirit face imprints. Some individuals, like Stevens, get frequent and dramatic results. The variables may boil down to subtle factors of consciousness and vibrational environmental conditions that presently are beyond our immediate ken and ability to control. But that's one of the goals of Macy's work – to discover how consciousness can have deliberate effect on the material, and on the intersections of dimensions.

Macy has had his own results: his deceased father, Blair, has appeared on several occasions. Some famous dead have made appearances as well as departed loved ones known only to the subjects. Among the famous are Albert Einstein, Edgar Cayce and Willis Harman, former president of the Institute for Noetic Sciences (IONS).

## Part of a big picture

Spirit face photography is a subset of ITC, which in turn is an outgrowth of electronic voice phenomena (EVP). In EVP, voices are recorded on tape or digital recorders; they are heard only during playback, not during recording. ITC involves more high-tech equipment, such as television sets, computers, faxes, telephones, apps and more; some of them enable real-time two-way EVP. ITC research has gone on around the world since the 1950s. It gained more public attention in the 1980s and 1990s, along with near-death experiences and after-death communications.

ITC is a partnership of dimensions. Higher beings, called ethereals, collaborate with deceased people, such as scientists, to form communication bridges with the living. Different spirit groups have been at work. They have their own team names, such as Timestream and Juno.

The ethereals are beings of a higher consciousness who are beyond form, said Macy. Some might use the term "angel" to describe them, though that label is far too limiting, and also is tied to religious associations. ITC transcends the boundaries of religions.

Overall, the ITC road has not been easy. The bridges cannot survive if human harmony is absent, for then there is no resonance with the higher realms. Resonance among researchers creates the right contact field. In recent years, infighting among researchers has caused some of the bridges to collapse.

The importance of consciousness makes ITC a modern alchemy. One could even call it the Great Work. Spiritual alchemy concerns enlightenment, the achievement of a fully integrated and purified human being. It emphasizes that success in this endeavor depends upon the spiritual consciousness of the individual. "It's attitude, attitude, attitude," agreed Macy about ITC. Those drawn to ITC research seem to have innate skills for it; Macy's spirit contacts told him he does. "The ethereals can see our thoughts and read our intentions," Macy said. He has had to work on his own purification as he has pursued the work.

## A life turning point

Macy entered ITC work as a result of confronting his own mortality. In 1988 he was diagnosed with colon cancer and found that his faith in the afterlife was not sufficient alone to convince him of survival. He needed more – he needed proof. "With death staring me in the face, I suddenly had to know about life after death," he said.

His research led him to meet leading experts, such as George Meek, an engineer who invented the Spiricom, a device that purportedly facilitated two-way conversations with the dead. Macy learned about EVP and achieved remarkable success with it. He also met international leaders in ITC, among them Maggy Harsch-Fischbach and Jules Harsch, a Luxembourg couple at the forefront of research. At the time, most of the best results were coming out of Europe and were documented in German. ITC changed his life.

Macy helped to form the International Network for Instrumental Transcommunication (INIT) in 1995, heading up the North American chapter. When INIT lapsed into dormancy – due in part to internal disagreements – Macy formed his own group, Worlditc.org, in 1998. He worked closely with ITC researchers, such as Rolf Erhardt of Ratingen, Germany, who in turn helped to get ITC data translated into English.

In the course of his work, Macy's cancer went into remission and he lost his fear of death. "ITC opened me up to a vast world – the world of spirit – that I didn't know existed," he said. "I'm not so immersed in the world of the material."

Macy was introduced to the luminator through therapist Jack Stucki of Colorado Springs, who used the luminator in his practice. Stucki's Polaroid photos, taken in therapy sessions, sometimes caught spirit faces as an added bonus. Macy saw immediate applications for ITC and knew he had to acquire one. He considers his luminator a gift from "the powers that be," the spiritual forces who guide him. He was led to the luminator with the understanding that he would not use it for paranormal displays and entertainment, but as a tool to serve The Project: to build solid evidence proving the realms of spirit, and to educate others.

## The Project

According to spirit communications, humans are a crossbreeding between primitive men on Earth and godlike superhumans of Eden, otherwise known as the planet Marduk, which once orbited between Mars and Jupiter. The inhabitants of Marduk blew up the planet by misusing their technologies. Marduk's marooned colonists on Earth established Atlantis, a super civilization which met the same fate, destroying itself with its own misused technology. A group of ethereals called The Seven came to Earth to help the survivors. Thus began The Project: to help humans regain their spiritual birthright.

Macy has been told by ethereals that six attempts at The Project have been undertaken since post-Atlantean times, and all have failed due to human failings. "There has always been a struggle between the two sides of human nature," Macy said. "The animal side is concerned with food, territory and mating rights. The spiritual side is concerned with ethics, values and services. As our evolution has advanced, both sides have become more powerful. But the dark side has always won out. The ethereals are hoping that the spiritual side will win."

The seventh attempt at The Project is now underway. If this one does not succeed, there is talk in the higher realms of abandoning it altogether, or at least for a long time, Macy said. Some of the best ethereal contacts have pulled back in the last five or six years, taking a wait-and-see stance. "They really want all of humanity to participate," he said. "Not just one or a few cultures."

Thus, the challenge: wake people up globally with evidence.

Can spirit faces help awaken people? Or is the luminator just another wrinkle in the long and troubled history of spirit photography?

## Real or fake?

People have been trying to capture spirit faces on film since the mid-19th century. Photographer William Mumler of Boston is credited with taking the first spirit photo – accidentally – when he sat for a self-portrait in 1861. Upon developing the photographic plate, he noticed what appeared to be the image of a dead person next to his. At the time, Spiritualism and communication with the dead were in vogue, and spirit photography shot up in popularity.

In early spirit photographs, ghostly faces of the "extras" float near portraits of the living. In some photographs, full-form spirits appear. But in order not to disappoint clients, unscrupulous photographers superimposed extras or created ghostly effects through double exposures. Many fraudulent photographs were accepted as real by an audience eager to communicate with dead loved ones or their spirit guides. Sometimes the extras turned out to be individuals very much alive.

More recently, thanks to the popularity of ghost-hunting books, television shows and films, the swelling ranks of paranormal investigators constantly attempt to capture images of ghosts at haunted sites. Most images have natural explanations, but some are anomalous.

The luminator spirit face photos have their critics. The blurring, they say, is caused by Macy moving the Polaroid camera, and perceiving faces in the photos is wish fulfillment and the human tendency to search for meaningful patterns.

Macy states that all of his spirit face photos are genuine, untouched and unaltered. "Nothing is contrived or faked," he said. He considers the photos proof of other realms, but leaves others to their own assessments, knowing that some will cling to skepticism no matter what. Everyone has their own "boggle point" past which they cannot go. However, boggle points do change as people are exposed more and more to new ideas and data.

For many of Macy's subjects, the proof is personal; they feel no need to convert the skeptical. Debbie Alberti, a professional singer in the Philadelphia area who lost her husband, John, attended one of Macy's workshops in the hopes of getting a spirit face photo, but she was skeptical that John would indeed come through. The results were undeniable, she said, erasing all doubt. Like others, Alberti became inspired to work for the ITC cause. "My inner world has opened up ten-fold in my understanding of other planes and worlds," she said. "I have cut out a lot of fear. My purpose is to help humanity understand the same."

Personal proof is important, but is nonetheless subjective, and thus is disregarded by science. Macy seeks to accomplish is the building of a stable model of spiritual reality that will influence the emergence of a new science.

Other streams of research are pointing in the same direction.

## Intentionality in a box

Psychokinesis, or the influence of mind over matter, has been demonstrated by test subjects in scientific experiments. Can human intention really be programmed and stored in a device such as the luminator? Research suggests that it can. Programmed intentionality is part of a new area of scientific research called "psychoenergetics."

A precursor to psychoenergetics was the work of Baron Karl von Reichenbach (1788-1869), a German chemist, metallurgist and expert on meteorites. Reichenbach was interested in the universal life force, a subtle energy that permeates all things in existence and governs health and life. He used the term "Od" to describe this force, and said it emanates from all things, including the stars and planets. Od especially streams from crystals, which can be seen as a kind of storage cell. (As noted, the liquid in the luminator acts like crystal.)

Reichenbach said Od can be observed by clairvoyants as luminous radiations similar to an aurora borealis and can be sensed as hot or cold. He also believed Od is affected by the breath, and that it fluctuates during the day and night, and before and after meals. Reichenbach's work was rejected by the scientific community, but in the late 19th century, the Society for Psychical Research in London validated many of his findings.

Wilhelm Reich (1897-1957), a native of Austria, a student of Freud and a psychoanalyst, coined the term "orgone" to describe a vital force or primordial cosmic energy as the basis of sex and psychosomatic neuroses. He agreed with Reichenbach that: this force permeates all things and existed as a biological energy; is blue in color; and can be demonstrated visually, thermically and electroscopically in the atmosphere with a Geiger counter. Reich practiced in the United States and developed a device called the "orgone accumulator," a metallic box covered with organic material which was supposed to concentrate orgone for therapeutic uses. He used the device on cancer patients and reported positive results. The Food and Drug Administration tested the device and pronounced it worthless. Reich was enjoined from manufacturing, distributing and using the device, and from using the term "orgone" in his writings. He refused. He was fined and sent to jail, where he died. The orgone accumulators were destroyed and his books were burned.

Physicist William Tiller has demonstrated that devices can indeed be programmed with intention via meditation, and, like batteries, have an effect upon material things. Tiller – known as "Dr. Bleep" for his appearance in the hit film *What the Bleep Do We Know?* – became interested in what he now calls psychoenergetics in the 1960s. His research has involved experienced meditators who program a specific intention into an "intentional imprinted electrical device," or IIED, a metal box charged with an electrical current. The energy stored within the IIED executes the intention, such as changing the pH or temperature of purified water. Furthermore, a programmed device imparts its stored intention into unprogrammed devices that are left in proximity of an IIED.

In his book *Some Science Adventures with Real Magic* (2005), Tiller states that "human consciousness, in the form of specific intentions, can have a robust effect on physical material property measurements for at least some inorganic and organic materials both in vitro and in vivo."

Tiller also allows for the participation of something spiritual beyond human beings. The meditators accomplished their intention programming "from a deep, collective meditation state, and perhaps with some unseen assistance," he said.

The device itself does not seem to be important. Tiller says that intention can be programmed into any objects. The key is consciousness.

This brings us back to the premise of the luminator: Intentional programming, perhaps combined with spiritual assistance, can be imparted to a device that somehow alters the physical environment so that faces of the dead and nonphysical beings are imprinted on film. The luminator is the real deal.

"The ethereals want us to learn about subtle energy and how to manipulate equipment with our thoughts," said Macy.

Once we succeed in that, we will truly be in a brave new world that will function according to new rules.

## The destiny ahead

In *Spirit Faces,* Macy outlines his views on the different dimensional realms and the afterlife, our spiritual history, our common purpose and our intended spiritual destiny. The soul is a piece of God, the Source and Center of everything. Our common purpose is to unite our consciousness and God self through prayer and meditation, to bring God's love and light into the world through us. Thus we restore ourselves to Paradise. Macy envisions a network of awakened "global visionaries" whose spiritual lights will be seen by the ethereals, who in turn will move ahead with The Project.

But if humans learn how to use their powers of mind, will they resist the temptation to wreak harm? In his book *The PK Man: A True Story of Mind Over Matter* (2000), Jeffrey Mishlove tells of his experiences with Ted Owens (d. 1987), who claimed to be able to manipulate the material world with his mind. He allowed his anger to affect his actions, and claimed to cause hurricanes, floods and even airplane crashes. Owens said he learned his skills from ETs.

Hopefully, the dark side of human nature will be transmuted and advances in spiritual consciousness will be accompanied by a collective desire to use power for good. Macy is confident that the spiritual will win out in the end. "Maybe it won't happen in my lifetime," he said, "but I can plant seeds."

*Rosemary Ellen Guiley: Author, researcher and Executive Editor of FATE.*

# CONTACT AND VISITATIONS
# FROM PETS

# THE ETERNAL BOND BETWEEN YOU AND YOUR PET
## Patti Roland

The death of a beloved pet is usually the most traumatic event in your relationship with that animal. Traumatic, yes, but perhaps there is a kernel of comfort in knowing that the loving relationship you have shared with your pet continues, even after your pet moves onto the spirit plane.

At some point after your pet's tenth year of life you may begin looking upon its advancing age with apprehension and misgiving. As your animal companion approaches its golden years, you will start observing physical changes in it. These include diminished ability to see and hear, the loss of teeth, the onset of tumors and a loss of control of bodily functions. As those changes occur, you become aware that your time of sharing the physical plane with your pet is getting shorter.

Be aware that your animal friend is tuned in to your thinking. For that reason, it is important to visualize the pet whole, healthy and fit.

Instead of letting the fear of losing the animal rule your mind and heart, send the animal your strong, positive vibrations.

With proper care, treatment, love and positive reinforcement, you can share many more fulfilling years with your pet. A pet can live a quality existence with diminished eyesight or hearing, fewer teeth and even weakened organs. What the animal needs, however, is a greater measure of love and understanding from his or her human companions.

If you continuously say (or think) such things as "Ginger is 12 years old; I know she won't be around much longer," or "Felix has lost control of his bodily functions; we'll have to put him to sleep one of these days," or "Ling won't make it to Christmas," your animal will do its best to accommodate what it interprets to be your wish that it die. The way your pet translates such messages is "I am getting old and sick and my owners don't want me around anymore."

Instead of sending signals of doom to your aging pet, give it messages like this: "I realize you are older than you once were, and that's okay with me. I love you and I will give you extra care and love. I want you to be with me until you determine it is time for you to leave your physical body."

When it's time for your pet to leave its body, it is important to realize that animals do not have the same attitudes and reactions to death that humans do. Animals are not as attached to their mortal forms as we are. They recognize when it is time for them to leave the physical plane and usually leave willingly, regardless of the apparent physical circumstances unfolding at that moment.

Although animals' spirits know when it is time to leave their bodies, they are sometimes reluctant to make the transition because they sense that their owners are unable to cope with their leaving. The pet often makes a conscious decision to remain on the physical plane until it gets a sign from its owner that it is okay to leave. For that reason, the pet often stays "here" far longer than it otherwise would – to the detriment of itself and of the humans who watch it deteriorate.

A pet owner who realizes that the time for the pet's transition is approaching can make the animal's departure easier. This can be done by speaking softly and gently to your pet, giving it permission to leave. Stroke or caress your pet as you speak in calm, soothing tones.

*Deceased pets often visit their owners.*

If you have been asked to make a decision about euthanasia for your pet, do not make it hastily. Take time to weigh the ramifications and alternatives. If you decide that euthanasia is the best action to take, sit quietly and hold your pet. Explain what is going to take place and why. Then, with your vet's permission, stay with your pet during the procedure, holding or touching the animal, speaking softly to it, reassuring it that you love it.

Once your pet has made its transition, allow yourself to feel your grief, your sense of loss. After all, you have just experienced the loss of a beloved family member. Don't allow others (even well-intended friends or relatives) to impose arbitrary time limits on your grieving process.

## Deeply felt loss

Many people don't understand that the loss of a pet can be felt as deeply as the loss of a human companion. Having experienced the death of a poodle and two Maltese, I know how painful it is to deal with such remarks as, "Go out and buy another animal right away." I could no

225

more go out and buy another dog right away than I could go out and buy another friend, brother or husband.

Your animal companion has the ability to re-embody. If you want the spirit of your pet to come back to you after its death, tell your pet so before it makes the transition. Then lovingly release your pet to its journey.

Pets usually reincarnate into the same loving relationship they left. Such direct reincarnations do not always occur immediately, especially if the pet's spirit has issues it needs to work on in the world of spirit.

It could be months before your pet's spirit returns to you. It might return in the same form as that of your departed pet, or it might choose a different species – it is entirely up to the animal's spirit.

It's not uncommon for a current pet to have one or more characteristics of a departed pet. Such a phenomenon is not surprising – the two animals are physical embodiments of the same spirit.

When your pet dies, the bond of love that connected you on the physical plane does not die. Such love is a beautiful and powerful ribbon woven through the dimensions, without beginning or ending.

That special love existed on the spirit plane before you and your animal companion came into each other's lives; it blossomed during your time together in physical form; it continues undiminished even after your pet enters the realm of spirit.

*Patti Roland: Freelance writer who specializes in animal awareness, interspecies communication and animal-owner interaction.*

FATE August 1994

# COMMUNICATION WITH YOUR DECEASED PET
## Eleanor Harris

Grieving the loss of your pet is a difficult process that can be eased greatly by remembering your pet in physical life and feeling the existing love between you that continues. Your loving relationship with your pet does not end at death but changes from a physical one to a spiritual one. Your pet's memory and love will bring you happiness for the rest of your life, and beyond. This is the divine promise of love.

Since 1993 I have worked with many pet lovers as a pet grief counselor. Most of the pet lovers come from diversified spiritual backgrounds with various beliefs concerning death, the afterlife, and spiritual communication. All have found comfort in practicing one form or another of spiritual communication with their deceased loved one.

Sara McNalley, a 54-year-old assistant manager, found coping with the death of her beloved collie, Max, especially difficult. "He struggled with cancer for over a year. I took him to specialists at the best veterinarian universities and hospitals. The veterinarians offered no hope. I had to make the difficult decision of euthanasia," she explains. "After his death, I battled with the grief and guilt. This led to depression. It wasn't until I actually tried to communicate with Max that I felt his undying love. I had been so worried that Max somehow hated me for taking his life although it was the humane thing to do. My guilt was immediately gone. I started resolving my grief right away. I felt like a new person."

When asked what she experienced during her first spiritual communication with Max, Sara explained, "I didn't know what to expect. As a devout Catholic, I believed that prayer was heard by Christ, the Virgin, and God, but I doubted whether or not communication with the deceased loved ones was possible. Using the meditation ritual, I connected with Max. I didn't see him in his physical body, but rather his soul, a body of light. I felt his immense love and devotion unchanged from how I felt it when he lived. The experience is hard to describe. I needed to know that I had done the right thing. I needed to know that he was free from suffering. I found all the answers that I was looking for."

## Loving Between the Worlds Meditation

This simple meditation ritual creates a bridge between our physical world and the spiritual world. Experiencing the bridge and meeting your pet can deepen your already existing bond. The loving connection through the bridge of communication is beautiful and empowering.

Sessions of communication with your pet can be as frequent as you desire. Though different from the physical contact with your pet, you will enjoy the energy-based interaction, which maintains its own beauty, sensations and ways to exchange love.

A spiritual relationship with your pet can change you as an individual. Through this spiritual dedication to your pet, you may feel a redirection of your life. His or her love for you, expressed now through bridged communication, strengthens you and helps make you a better individual.

**What You Will Need:** Your favorite flowers, photographs of you and your pet, your pet's belongings, candles and crystals to decorate the space where you will practice the mediation. Matches, incense to help obtain a meditative state (sweetgrass works well), and a quiet melody of music.

**Preparations:** Decorate a table for your pet, using the flowers, candles, crystals, photographs and your pet's belongings, making a type of sanctuary for your pet. You can use the objects on the table to help focus your mind on your pet before starting the meditation. Dress comfortably. Darken the area using the candles for illumination.

## How to Perform the Meditation Ritual

Begin by casting your circle, or ritually opening your sacred space as normally done in your religious practice.

Lie on your back with your knees bent so that your feet are flat on the floor. Begin relaxing every part of your body, starting with your feet and ending with your head. Tensing and relaxing each muscle group is a good way to assure total body relaxation. Repeat this procedure if necessary. Feel grounded through the pressure of your feet against the earth. Energy can be felt moving upward from your feet and through your entire being and exiting out the top of your head. You are centered, and deeply relaxed.

Meditate, allowing your conscious mind to rest as deeper levels of your unconscious mind unfold. Focus your will to the intent of communicating with your beloved pet. When you feel ready, ask your pet to appear to you. If you experience a block when attempting to communicate with your pet, ask for his or her help. Draw energy up from the earth, through your feet, and release it through your crown chakra at the top of your head. This will clear your chakras and prompt clarity within your aura.

When your pet appears, look at it. What does it look like? Is your pet in bodily form or in an energy form? Ask what it needs from you. Ask how it is easiest for you to contact it. Are there other beings present with your pet – other animals, spirit guides, and so on? Is there someone else who wishes to come forward to communicate? Ask whatever questions you want answered at this initial communication. Provide time between each question for your pet to send you answering messages. The communication process should be slow paced.

Once you've asked initial questions and have communicated with your pet long enough, send love through your aura and say a temporary farewell. Come out of the meditation slowly. Return gently, allowing your conscious mind to awaken.

Offer thanks to the divine for making the communication with your beloved pet possible. Close your circle or sacred space. You may desire to ground yourself of residual energy by eating food. You may even desire to have a snack within your sacred space and reflect on your wonderful interaction with your pet.

## Change Your Life

Your memory of the special spiritual relationship with your pet can change you as an individual. You may actually feel as if you've become a different person. You may feel a redirection of your life through spiritual dedication to your pet. The joy, learning and exchanging of love and living with your pet has enriched your life and will benefit you forever. His or her love for you, expressed now through bridged communication, strengthens you and helps make you a better individual.

Please do not rush resolution. The healing process takes patience and time and gradually will make you stronger. Don't become frustrated with yourself. This can drastically slow your recovery. What you make of your life now as you pick up the pieces is exercising what you were given by that special bond with your pet and is the ultimate testimony of your shared love.

How you envision your reunion with your pet is a unique, intimate experience. You may sense your pet's presence or visualize him or her.

*Eleanor Hanis: Author and grief counselor for pet loss.*

FATE May 2000

# "I CAME BACK FOR MY DOG"
## Barbara C. Powell

As a professional psychic I am interested in the many kinds of paranormal experiences people report. One of the most unusual incidents I have ever heard of occurred in Wendover, Utah, in January 1963.

Joe Benson was a spiritual leader to the Goshute Indians. One day, while visiting one of the local markets in Wendover, he found a stray puppy, weak and pitiful but full of the life spirit. Recognizing this as a bond between them, the old man took the dog home.

He nursed it on venison broth and mixtures of native herbs which healed and strengthened the animal. Then, as the dog got better, he named him Sky because in his culture the sky held the greatest strength. Soon the old man and his dog could be seen making regular rounds from the high sheep meadows to the corrals where the younger men of the family broke horses for neighboring ranchers.

By the time the winter came to the pine and sage country, the dog had grown to become a magnificent German shepherd of apparently pure lineage. Sky had only one master. He was reserved and rarely friendly with others; he loved only the old man who had saved him. As Mr. Benson grew older and his vision failed him, the dog guarded his steps. His family worried about him because they sensed that more than his eyes had weakened. Still, they felt sure that Sky would watch him and keep him from harm.

Finally, Joe Benson went to his wife, Mable, and announced that his time was near. She sent word to the relatives. The children, grandchildren, nephews and nieces all came to the old man's bedside. Because they were more involved in white society than he was, they ignored his protests and insisted he be moved to the Indian Hospital in Owyhee, Nevada. Sky growled when they lifted him and cried when they took him away.

The old man did not last long in the hospital. He asked that the nurses place him in a chair each day so that he could look down the valley in the direction of his home. At last, knowing that Joe Benson was beyond their care, they sent him home to Wendover to die. In deep winter, in January 1963, he died.

The funeral celebration lasted several days. Singers came and sang to his soul for three nights. Other wise and holy men came to contribute their chants. Finally, at the dawning of the fourth day, the people were sure that his soul had passed beyond. Quietly they ate the huge breakfast that was prepared for them and just as quietly they left. Soon only Mable was left in the house, alone with her memories and Joe's dog Sky.

Before they left the little town in Utah, several persons, children, grandchildren and the old man's friends, had asked for the dog. The old woman thought about it. The dog, which seemed to be grieving even more than she was, filled the house with his sorrow but she sensed that that would be the wrong thing to do. So, she kept the dog.

About 10 days later she happened to look out the window to see a man coming up her road. She built up the fire in her old cookstove and put on the coffee for her guest. The coffee was just heating up when she saw her visitor in the doorway. Her hand trembled but she did not drop the coffeepot. She placed it on the stove and turned back to face him. It was Joe.

232

True to the traditions of her people, she gently explained to him that he was dead, that he had no business in the land of the living and that he had to pass on. This world was closed to him.

Joe nodded. "I am going," he said. "I came back for my dog." He whistled and called and Sky came running into the kitchen. He wagged his tail, then sat down expectantly. "I want his leash," Joe said to Mable.

Mable went to a hook on the wall and took it down. She handed it to him, making sure that she did not touch him.

Grandfather snapped the leash on Sky's collar and led the dog away, across the porch, down the steps and along the familiar path around the hill. Not once did he turn back even to wave to his wife; not once did he say goodbye.

Mable hesitated for a moment, then ran after him. When she reached the turn of the hill and looked, there was nothing. Joe and Sky were gone.

Joe and Mable's daughter, Arvilla Benson Urban, who lived next door to them, saw this happen and has sworn to it in an affidavit sent to FATE. In late January 1963, Arvilla said, "I saw my father enter the house and not more than a few minutes later I saw him leave with the dog on a leash. I saw my mother go after him and I, after I could think, went after her. When I reached the top of the hill, my father and his dog were gone."

The young men of the family spent several days searching for the dog. No trace of him or of his leash was ever found.

All of those who had asked for the dog were later thankful that they hadn't taken him. They would not have wanted Joe to come to their house asking for Sky.

FATE June 1986

# THE KITTEN CAME FOR PHIL
## Alice Morgan

My brother, Phil D'Amico, was 8-¼ years old when he died of leukemia on July 11, 1966. He had suffered the ravages of the disease with incredible bravery and maturity and often expressed his innocent, deeply moving faith that he would continue to live after death.

His third-grade classmates, in an attempt to bring him some pleasure, took up a collection to buy Phil a darling little orange Persian kitten. But the gift came too late. The kitten arrived as we returned to our Yonkers, New York home after having laid little Phil to rest.

Our parents, exhausted and grief-stricken, were not keen on having a pet and asked the pet shop delivery man to take the kitten back, explaining that Phil had passed on. The delivery man had the kitten in his arms when suddenly it squirmed loose, jumped to the floor and dashed wildly up the stairs to the second-floor bedrooms. With a hurried apology the man rushed after the cat. In what had been Phil's room he cornered the animal. The kitten was crouched at the head of the bed, claws firmly anchored in Phil's pillow. When my parents saw the pleading look in the kitten's eyes, they couldn't resist; they agreed to keep him after all.

We called him Phil's Kitty which, after a while, was shortened to Skitty. And the little animal took his place as a family member in no time at all. Somehow, he seemed like Phil, extremely affectionate and gently playful. As the months passed, we could not fail to notice there was something quite unusual about Skitty, and although we did not often talk about it, we all came to suspect that Phil was trying to communicate with us through the kitten.

Skitty insisted on sleeping in Phil's now empty room, and repeated attempts to take him out brought forth endless pitiful wailing. At 3:15 each afternoon, the time when Phil would have come home from school, the kitten appeared in the kitchen to beg for a snack. It had been Phil's habit to have milk and cookies every afternoon at that very hour.

The truly incredible event that turned our suspicions into unshakable belief occurred the following November on the day that would have been Phil's ninth birthday. Skitty was now about seven or eight months old. On that day Skitty suddenly appeared in the front yard of the Mallory home.

Jimmy Mallory had been Phil's best friend. The cat was rolling Phil's pink rubber ball along with his little furry paws. Jimmy's home was a full two blocks away. How the cat traversed that distance, dodging traffic and maneuvering the ball up and down curbs, was beyond our comprehension. And how could he have known Jimmy's house?

Jimmy's mother was raking leaves in the front yard when she spotted Skitty. Knowing that he never strayed from our yard, she called us immediately. We were stunned, for we hadn't even noticed that Skitty was missing. The cat had been playing with Phil's ball under our oak tree – but now he seemed to be indicating that Jimmy was to have the ball. What better way to celebrate Phil's birthday?

Other incidents through the years reaffirmed our belief that Phil was indeed "alive" and speaking to us through Skitty. In May 1974 the cat, now eight years old, started to lose weight. The vet diagnosed feline lymphosarcoma – a fatal disease similar to the one that took Phil. There was no cure, no treatment. We tried to make Skitty's last days as comfortable as possible, and like Phil, the cat tolerated the illness with dignity. He purred when he was stroked up until the day he died – July 11, 1974, eight years to the day after Phil's death.

Later that year I married John Morgan and moved to my own home in a nearby town. I had developed a deep admiration and love for cats, but we did not have one because my husband is allergic to cat dander. One evening the following summer I awoke in the middle of the night to the sound of a cat leaping onto my bed. There is an odd half-muffled "mrrr" that cats "say" as they land after leaping; it is an unmistakable sound. I was startled but I didn't want to wake my husband. I reached out in the darkness and felt a long-haired cat about the size and fluffiness of Skitty. I felt for the ears. One had a V-shaped notch, just as Skitty had had. It was incredible!

My husband, apparently awakened by my movements and sharp intake of breath, sat up and switched on the light. As he did so, the feeling of a cat under my hand vanished. I told him what had happened, but he passed it off as a dream. I knew it wasn't a dream, but I didn't argue.

The next morning as I was making the bed I found several orange-buff cat hairs on my pillow, exactly the color of Skitty's fur. There had been a cat in my bedroom the night before. I looked at the calendar. The date was July 11.

FATE September 1980

# About FATE Magazine

Six decades before reality TV shows and late-night radio's *Coast to Coast AM*, and countless websites, blogs, books, and movies began captivating audiences with true tales of UFOs and the paranormal – there was FATE – a first-of-its-kind publication dedicated to in-depth coverage of mysterious and unexplained phenomena.

FATE was a true journalistic pioneer, covering issues like electronic voice phenomena, life on Mars, telepathic communication with animals, and UFOs at a time when discussing such things was neither hip nor trendy. Today FATE enjoys a rare longevity achieved by only a select few US periodicals.

## How it all began

The year was 1948. The Cold War was in its infancy, and the Space Age was still a dream... but across the nation and around the world, people observed strange objects flying through the skies.

Two Chicago-based magazine editors, Raymond A. Palmer and Curtis B. Fuller, took a close look at the public's fascination with flying saucers and saw the opportunity of a lifetime. With help from connections in the worlds of science fiction and alternative spirituality, they launched a new magazine dedicated to the objective exploration of the world's mysteries. They gave their "cosmic reporter" the name FATE.

FATE's first issue, published in Spring 1948, featured as its cover story the first-hand report of pilot Kenneth Arnold on his UFO sighting of the previous year, an event widely recognized by UFO historians as the birth of the modern UFO era.

## FATE's ongoing coverage of survival after death

FATE has covered a wide range of topics during its lifetime. From the beginning, it has provided steady coverage of survival after death and related topics, such as near-death experiences, mediumship, dreams and communication with the dead. Every issue of FATE – more than 730 to date – has included personal testimonies of experiences that have convinced people that death is not the end.

## Relevant today

In a fast-paced, high-tech world that is often short on attention span and long on cynicism, how does a magazine like FATE continue to thrive? Editor-in-Chief Phyllis Galde says, "FATE allows readers to think for themselves by providing them with stories that mainstream publications don't dare touch. The truth is, reality does not conform to the neat and tidy box that many people would like to wedge it into. Our world is a bizarre and wondrous place and our universe is filled with mystery – it is teeming with the unknown. People are longing for something more than the mundane transactions of everyday existence. FATE feeds the soul's appetite for the enigmatic, the esoteric, and the extraordinary."

## Subscribe to FATE

FATE is published in intervals throughout the year in a popular digest size. Join the family of subscribers by visiting the FATE website at www.fatemag.com.

# About Rosemary Ellen Guiley

Rosemary Ellen Guiley, Executive Editor of FATE magazine, is a leading expert in the metaphysical and paranormal fields, with more than 65 books published on a wide range of paranormal, UFO, cryptid, spiritual and mystical topics, including nine single-volume encyclopedias and reference works. Her work focuses on interdimensional entity contact experiences of all kinds (spirit, alien, creature), the afterlife and spirit communications, contact with extraterrestrials, aliens and nonhuman intelligent beings, problem hauntings, spirit and entity attachments, psychic skills, dreamwork for well-being, spiritual growth and development, angels, past and parallel lives, and investigation of unusual paranormal activity. She has worked full-time as an investigator, researcher, author, and presenter since 1983, and spends a great deal of time in the field doing original research.

Rosemary is president and owner of Visionary Living, Inc., a publishing and media company; its publishing division is Visionary Living Publishing, specializing in nonfiction and fiction books on paranormal and metaphysical topics. Visit www.visionarylivingpublishing.com.

## A personal note from Rosemary

I have been privileged to be part of the FATE family since 1991-92. Dennis Stillings, the publisher of *Artifex* magazine, introduced me to Phyllis Galde and David Godwin, editors of FATE. They invited me to contribute to the magazine, and a lasting friendship was struck.

I started as a columnist, joining a prestigious company of other FATE columnists and regulars, among them John A. Keel, Mark Chorvinsky, Loyd Auerbach, Antonio Huneeus, and Loren Coleman.

In the early 2000s, Phyllis and David purchased FATE from Llewellyn Worldwide Publications. David passed in 2012, and FATE remains under Phyllis's ownership.

Over the course of time, I went from columnist to consulting editor, and in 2016 became Executive Editor, taking on more editing responsibilities. Phyllis and I entered into a partnership to publish a series of books on the best from the archives of FATE on timeless topics of ongoing interest. FATE has thousands of excellent articles in its vaults, written by the best of the best, and I am pleased to make many of them available again.

.td.

)02B/653/P

9 781942 157359